AUTISM SUPERHEROES

THE SPARK WITHIN

NIKI HUMM

Copyright © 2018

All rights reserved. This book or any portion thereof may not be reproduced or used in any manner whatsoever without the express written permission of the author except for the use of brief quotations in a book review.

Printed in Australia
First Printing, 2018
ISBN: 978-0-6484104-9-2

White Light Publishing House
Melton, VIC, Australia 3337
whitelightpublishing.com.au

For Cambo & Pumba

Dedicated to

Les and Debbie Humm

Contents

Preface — 11

Chapter One — 19
Delays, Challenges and Labels
(the beginning of our story)

Chapter Two — 27
The Soul

Chapter Three — 33
You are the Chosen One
(Why Self-Care is Crucial. How to find your Zen.)

Chapter Four — 47
Mother's Intuition:
The bond between mother and child

Chapter Five — 61
Father-child bond
(and non-biological father connections)

Chapter Six — 77
Integrity, Time, Patience, Respect.

Chapter Seven — 95
Therapists, Courses and You (Oh My!)

Chapter Eight 111
Making Sense of Sensory Processing

Chapter Nine 121
Outside the Box Communication – Part One

Chapter Ten 141
Outside the Box Communication – Part Two

Chapter Eleven 149
The View – Part One

Chapter Twelve 157
The View – Part Two
Energy Layers 159
Energy Hubs 181

Chapter Thirteen 197
What is 'High Frequency' – really?

Chapter Fourteen 211
Grounding

Chapter Fifteen 223
Anchoring

Chapter Sixteen 239
Siblings are Superheroes too

Addendum 249

A Parting Word from the Author 269

This book is for you if:

- You're a parent or carer of someone with an Autism diagnosis.
- You care for, teach or simply love someone on The Spectrum.
- Awareness that this book relates (but not limited to) high functioning levels of Autism and is predominately relating to those on The Spectrum between 3 and 11 years old as (from 2018 onwards.)
- You are interested in the journey of others on a similar path.
- You have an open mind regarding your perspectives and perceptions of spirituality, healing and topics of a metaphysical nature.
- You deeply care about connection and are looking for perspectives that may not be considered mainstream.
- You are not looking for the "cause" of Autism, but alternative perspectives about the condition.

This book is NOT for you if:

- You have no interest in Autism and Sensory needs.
- You have strict limitations as to what you are willing to believe about spirituality and healing.
- You are not interested in reading about another person's journey.
- You are looking for a reason for the Autism Diagnosis.
- You are looking to "cure" Autism.

Welcome

Thank you for your interest and your time in reading this book. I trust you will find something useful or meaningful within these pages.

Preface

Autism. It's everywhere... We've all heard about it. We're aware of the stigmas attached to the label and the sense of fear it stirs within parents globally. **What if I were to tell you that it's just that – a label?** What if I told you your child is perfect. Your child is healthy. Your child is unique, and creative, and intelligent. Would you believe me? How does that make you feel, to think of your child as perfect – just the way they are now? Do you feel the lump rising in your throat as tears well in your eyes?

In your heart of hearts, you know it's true. Don't get me wrong, even though it's just a label – Autism is very real to those who live it. To those who have the diagnosis and to those who support them, oh yes... it is very, very real. Sometimes I think these Souls are the most authentic and real you can get. It seems at times we can't handle the depth of their reality, or the scope of their potential.

At times, they can't handle ours either.

My aim for this book, is to share the most relevant parts of my story – about how I came to believe and receive energetic information about this mysterious condition. Through my story and my unique perspective and experience, I hope to provide you with an alternative - something different that may just strike a chord with you. I hope to give you something you can resonate with, things that feel familiar or true… to show you, you are not alone. To appreciate you for being here.

I know dear, beautiful Soul – you have read anything and everything in the hope you can help or understand your little one better… and here you are, loving some more. That is why he/she chose you, because you are willing to do the hard yards, you are loving this little person so much – that you are desperately trying to find something, anything to ease their burden. You are searching for anything that might give them a chance at a 'normal' life, or for you to be able to understand them just that little bit better.

Bless you, dear heart. I hope you know just how strong, beautiful and resilient you are.

Let me set the precedent by saying right here, at the start – keep your mind and heart open as you read on. *Feel* your way through this book. It is not a medical journal. It is not based on science, nor statistics – it is based on one mother's account and anecdotes, her empathy and her voice from her own experiences. I am certainly not a doctor – but I am the only one in the world who experiences things the way that I do. (Just as you too, are the only one who experiences your reality.) I am real, my children are real, and our stories are true.

Even before I had children, I seemed to come across children with Autism – and we gravitated towards one another. When I was nineteen years old I was fortunate enough to have lived with a family who had a child on The Spectrum, who has taught me so much more than any book or course ever could. That period in my life gave me insight not only into the Soul with the diagnosis – but the extreme impact it had on his family.

I witnessed the extreme exhaustion of his parents - constantly trying, and consistently and immensely accepting and loving. I saw siblings who had to adapt, to understand and to help. The child and I - we seemed to have our own language, and we shared an amazing bond. That family won't be the basis of this book however, as I will mostly draw anecdotes from the deepest crevasse of my heart – my own little family and our Autism journey together.

My first born is on The Spectrum, but that doesn't define him. It helps to explain that he is of high frequency, or in layman's terms – refer to society's label that he is 'not a typically developing child'. He is my muse, my inspiration to want to help others like him, and others like us – his family. I refer to him in this book as 'My Precious'. (His baby brother 'My Little Precious'.) Autism seems to attract pity and awkwardness, possibly an element of fear – for what people don't understand scares them.

My boy teaches me more than I teach him - every day. He outsmarts me, every day. He finds a way to surprise me – always. Most of all, his 'lovable' factor grows by the minute, as he navigates the world in his unique way. His way is different - trying, exhausting, but absolutely fucking beautiful. **We don't need pity, we need understanding and acceptance.**

Keep in mind, my child is quite high functioning and my story will be different to yours. However, I'm sure we can relate in a lot of ways, and my mission is to reach you. The rest is up to you. **Thank you for connecting with me. I trust this helps you in some magical way.** What makes this book any different to any other story? Aside from my random bouts of Aussie humour and uncensored style of writing (you're welcome, by the way) I have a bizarre and unorthodox view. I am writing not just as a parent, but as a Spiritual Channel - a vessel for divine information.

There are many names for what I do, such as Intuitive, Psychic/Medium, Energy Worker… (you get the idea). Lucky for me I am 'coming out' in an energy that accepts such gifts, and you may well be in tune with yours too. I like to think I am just a normal person, but I am also a Warrior for the Light – everything I do and work toward is possible because of my connection to Source. I allow Spirit to work through me. Some of this book will be based on spiritual information - channelled straight from the Divine as an unfiltered powerful force – some insights and explanations that I have no way of knowing otherwise.

Some of my anecdotes will be practical; learned information and skills put into practice after years of therapies and research. Other things may be completely metaphysical, spiritual and to the closed mind – seem a bunch of hog-wash. All the while – my experiences are shared with you with love, in hopes that it may resonate with you on a Soul level. I trust that you and your child (the one who has you reading this) are somehow going to benefit from the seeds that are being planted into your subconscious and conscious mind.

I am sharing my insights as someone who has been where you are (in some ways). I am someone who will always continue to dig deeper, find better ways to help My Precious, and those in the collective consciousness who have similar struggles. Do I have all of the answers? Nope, sorry. I wish I did. Am I a perfect parent? Absolutely not. But I am real.

My job here is to share what I have learned, and hopefully give you something you need. My job here is to help those beautiful high frequency children to be understood and help them to thrive and flourish. **Let me tell you a secret...** Your child, the one with the labels, the guinea pig for the tests and hoop-jumps and judgements – the child who society may think is weird or odd or will amount to nothing - is very, very important. That child is divinely appointed here, right now – as we all are. Your mission is to help them.

But you already know that, don't you?

Affirmation

My experience is unique.

I give thanks for my unique experience,

for it makes up the pages that create my story.

I honour my feelings.

My feelings are valid and real.

I allow myself to flow with ease and grace

I see the perfection within each moment.

I trust the process, even when I may not understand the details yet.

I AM BLESSED.

I AM PEACEFUL.

Chapter One

**Delays, Challenges and Labels
(the beginning of our story)**

Let's assume that your child (or the one who you have in mind as you read this book) has been under the microscope since the beginning. Your beautiful baby, your precious little bean has blossomed from a tiny baby into an energizer bunny, a bouncing toddler. He or she perhaps isn't quite meeting their developmental milestones and appears to respond 'differently' to stimuli when compared to your friend's children or your other children (if there are siblings).

You might have 'known' immediately that something was different, or some sort of alarm bells were ringing because you've read about this, you know the warning signs. You panic. Something inside you refuses to admit that there is anything 'wrong' with your Precious one – they are and will always be perfect in your eyes (because of course, they are). At your next health check or Maternal Child Health appointment you notice the answers to the questions asked seem to have alarmed not only you, but the nurse as well. Not to stir panic, they tell you to '"See how it goes, boys are late bloomers". But you know something – don't you? You feel it in your gut.

Moving along, you're sent for screening tests, assessments that monitor your child's ability for speech, movement, socialisation skills, temperament, body language. You watch as your child is judged so harshly – making excuses in your mind as to the reason why your child may not have 'performed' the way they otherwise would have. "Oh, he's tired, he's always unresponsive when he's tired." "Oh, she's just shy around strangers, she's not like that at home with me."

At his first Occupational Therapy and Speech Screening, I felt my Precious was a tiny little bug under the microscope, squirming and confused - looking to me for help to get those eyes off him. Looking at me like, "Why won't you save me, Mummy?" I felt hurt for him. I wanted to take him away and keep him safe from judgement – safe from being compared to 'typically developing children' where he was just a 'normal' happy child. Seeing him in a clinical play-based setting among other children was eye-opening… and it was heart wrenching.

The therapist sat with us briefly afterwards to explain her results, and what she said (and cleverly *didn't* say) made me want to shove her little pen right down her throat. I don't have a mean bone in my body, by the way. Mumma-bear was rearing onto her hind legs at the cold judgement about her Precious. Within five minutes she rattled off a bunch of 'failures to' and 'not applicable'. I felt as though she was telling me my son was an alien, or that he was stupid.

It hurt, to think that someone who had spent years at school being educated on the subject – could sit there and tell me so blatantly that she knew more about him than I did, that he was imperfect in *any* way. She insisted he was not reaching his milestones. He was severely delayed. She told me what he should be able to do but couldn't. My blood boiled, as I tried to keep him calm. He was utterly exhausted, and he just wanted to get the hell out of there.

I was reeling. "Who the heck are you? You don't know my child better than I do! Who sets these bloody milestones? And do they take into account that my child is the happiest, most carefree kid in the world – usually? He's just uncomfortable right now because he KNOWS you're all judging him!" Of course, these thoughts stayed trapped in my head – as I could barely muster a sound. I was angry because underneath it all, I was hurt. You know what I mean, don't you? That feeling that you don't want to admit it, nor do you want to believe it or acknowledge it… It sucks, it really sucks.

What the professionals do is necessary of course and works toward a greater good – but it doesn't feel like it at the time. Your natural animal instinct is to protect your young, and the threat of someone accusing your child of being anything less than perfect is bound to get you wound up. Hopefully, you realise that this instinctual reaction is normal. But at the same time – the results are in and emotions aside - you know there's a long road of tireless work ahead.

Whatever you felt or continue to feel about this is *your* normal – there is no right or wrong way to feel. Like anything, it's a process, and we all process things our own way. I can't even count on two hands and two feet how many of these types of appointments we attended in my child's first three years. People in my social circles and family would ask me if I would return to work anytime soon. It was hard to explain to them that I had a full-time job: secretary, chauffer, security guard, advocate, avid 'minutes' keeper, interpreter, punching bag. Not to mention running a household and being a wife.

My Precious was intensely aggressive, so as if these appointments weren't stressful enough - the harsh reality I faced was being a human punching bag. I was the only thing between him and the busy car park, or the hard floor, or the walls, or his own fists and feet. **My body was the recipient of the frustration my child was going through.** I supported countless black eyes, fat lips, injured shoulders and ribs from carrying a kicking child (who was clearly stronger than he looked) or from hugging my baby amid a sensory overload so as he didn't hurt himself.

I became so overwhelmed at times that my child had such terrifying screaming fits, such aggressive outbursts, just all in all such a fucking horrible time of it... and yet when we were at home he was (for the most part) a little angel. At home, in his safe space – he was free to just be himself without judgement. I often wished I could avoid the therapy appointments; it was emotionally and physically demanding on both of us. It took away the time to just bond with my child; instead of making playdough in our PJs we were attending yet another clinical appointment.

Although he began to enjoy it and look forward to the playtime with his therapists (who became familiar 'friends') he still couldn't handle waiting in that room for more than a few minutes. He still kicked the crap out of my seat and screamed bloody murder if I parked in a different spot than last time. He still didn't want to give up that activity he so thoroughly enjoyed when it was time to go. **That was just one aspect of our lives at the time.** Grocery shopping was a nightmare. Visiting friends was exhausting.

My husband at the time and I never had date nights – because who could we possibly trust to take care of our child? Importantly, we knew no one qualified to deal with his needs – because the slightest little change in his routine could have him hysterical and having a meltdown that they couldn't possibly handle. Sleep. What was that? Having struggled for years to get him to sleep through the night (this took six years and is still temperamental) it became part of my life that I would need to get up at least two times a night to either settle him again or drag him into my arms and calm him to sleep with me in a deep pressure bear hug. This was all PRIOR to an official diagnosis, mind you.

When the time came, I already knew. I just desperately wanted confirmation. Confirmation of what I was truly dealing with – to make a real difference in his life and to make sure I was using the appropriate strategies and doing the right courses. I've heard a lot of people try to avoid the assessment, and this is totally understandable. Me? I *welcomed* the diagnosis. Although I was emotional about it, for sure… I was relieved. I now had a REASON for the things we were going through, and I could make plans for his future, knowing what direction to head in.

The official diagnosis was 'Autism Spectrum Disorder' with severe Sensory Processing issues. I already knew that, because like you I'm sure – I researched the shit out of everything. Although this was a label slapped onto my child – forcing him into a societal category and limiting his potential by default… it was necessary for me to get him the help he so desperately needed. It was a golden ticket to explain 'why' I didn't just yell and scream at my 'brat' or give him a smack on the backside for being 'naughty'.

The label wasn't for him…it was for me.

My child is still perfect. The diagnosis couldn't change a thing about him; my beautiful, remarkable little Precious. The 'label' was useful for me to use in the society we live in, and to get the best out of the resources and facilities around us in order to truly make a difference while he was little – to give him the best start in a holistic and meaningful way.

So, if you're struggling with the diagnosis at this time, or can relate to my story here – just know that although it feels awful to have to categorise your Precious one(s), or if it feels like they will be seen as different or not-accepted… these feelings are certainly valid and real.

My advice at this juncture: make it work for you, for your Precious.

I like to see it as a uniqueness, for who is to say what is really 'normal' anyway? It is a 'different-ability' not a 'disability'. Your child is always going to be your child, who loves you and who you love immensely. Nothing, no simple word or label on a spectrum of labels is ever going to change that.

Affirmation

My child is Divine Perfection.

I am Divine Perfection.

Together we are strong.

Our love can move mountains.

Chapter Two

The Soul

From the suspected inkling that there may be traits of Autism in your child (or significant other, maybe even yourself) – to wherever you are at right now… one thing needs to be ascertained before continuing forward in this book. It is integral that from the get-go – whatever work you intend on carrying out with this person or whatever help you wish to provide for them, that you understand who you're really dealing with.

Underneath all labels, all physical characteristics, all abilities and diff-abilities, all personality…

WHO DO YOU *THINK THEY* ARE?

WHO DO YOU *THINK YOU* ARE?

Who are you, really? *Have a think about what your answer is to that, before proceeding.* Are you a person? Sure. A human person. Are you a body? Sure, sure. You HAVE a body. **But who are you?** I bet you naturally want to reply with the fundamental characteristics of your human form; what you do, how many children you have, your personality type and all of those types of things.

What I want you to think about, is who are you underneath your shell?

Your body is your vessel, carrying and enacting the part of 'the brains' underneath. No, you're not a brain (although that's very handy to have); you're so much more than thought and physical being. If you can, imagine the brightest star in the night sky, sparkling with all things pretty and shiny. Picture that light as it pulsates and expands light into the darkness around it. It has an ambiance, a brilliance. It draws you in with its shimmering warmth and the feeling of love emanating from it.

Beautiful, isn't it?

That star, that spark – that is who you truly are. You are a Soul. A Divine Spark. The essence of everything you are and everything you are about – is all in there. The exterior is the encasing that acts out your role on the stage that is life here on Earth, but truly you are a Soul. **A beautiful, pure light of love and peace. That is who you are.** That is who I am. That is who everyone truly is, underneath. Your Soul contains many lifetimes of cellular memory, cosmic information, divine knowledge and so much more. Your Soul has its own life force that stores within it more information than you can even begin to comprehend. But at the crux of it – the warm gooey centre is peace and love.

That is your natural state, that is who you are.

Now let's go back to your Precious child or children – the one who has you loving them enough to read this book. THEY are Souls too. A divine spark. A physical manifestation of pure peace and love. Can you see them? When you look at them, can you see their light? With every interaction, someone on the spectrum can SEE your light. If you are trying to communicate with someone on the Spectrum and all you see in them are challenges, physical differences, self-stimulating mannerisms or tics…

If all you see is someone who doesn't think cognitive thought because they can't speak…do you think their beautiful sparkling Soul will trust you? Will they let you into their world?

They say children are brutally honest. Do you know why? Because they are still aware that they are a Soul. They are not yet limited by the restrictions of society and what's deemed acceptable behaviour. **They call it as they see it. They live by heart and imagination, innocence and curiosity.**

Child-like wonder is something we adults often wish we still possessed or must force ourselves to allow time and space to tap into. We are all born knowing what we are here for and that we are Souls having a human experience… we have just forgotten. A child or person on The Spectrum – no matter what age, may be labelled as having the maturity of a smaller child. Oh, how incredibly awesome that must be, right? For them, the Soul – they may not fit into society's rules of how they should be – but boy I bet they have a spectacular view of the world!

So now that you're contemplating The Soul – and that we are all Souls having another human experience (most likely it's not our first rodeo), be aware that we have each undertaken a Divine Assignment to be here. Each of us has chosen (or been given) a set mission or task to complete during our time here – whether it be a short time or a long time. Many are on mission to simply raise the frequency, to widen the dimensions of which our current society views things. Many are here to bring in new energy, to anchor light into the planet or into the Collective Consciousness.

There are ample reasons for **being**. There are countless 'meanings' to our lives, each one unique and different to the next person. Yet here we all are together. You, The Soul – are here helping and loving this other Soul and many others for a reason. You chose to. You chose each other. Moving forward, challenges and hardships included – you The Soul, whatever your specific mission is…

You've got this.

Affirmation

I am Peace.

I am Love.

I am not this body.

I am not this personality.

I am not my circumstances.

I am a Divine Shining Light.

I am a pure and divine spark.

I AM A SOUL

Chapter Three

You are the Chosen One
(Why Self-Care is Crucial. How to find your Zen.)

Whatever your role in the lives of those around you – is important. It is Divine. It is meaningful. Do you ever feel like a failure? Or that you're not living up to the task? As a parent, I constantly judge and ridicule myself for my mistakes and my short-comings. I'm certainly not alone in this, and I think that every loving parent who ever lived has had trouble accepting their own choices at some point or other.

Why do we beat ourselves up incessantly?

Because on some level, whether we consciously chose to become parents or care givers in this lifetime or we feel the responsibility was thrust upon us, we all know deep down that we were *chosen* to achieve this task. We have a job to do, and we feel like we're not doing it well enough. We compare ourselves and compete against each other in a bid to feel as though we are winning at this game, or at least 'good enough' to compete. The truth is, the people we compare ourselves to are just as lost and exhausted as we are.

We weren't given a handbook on the rules, the boundaries and the possibilities (not a tangible, physical one anyway.) We could never truly prepare for the array of overwhelming feelings of love, pride, joy; and not forgetting the immense, consuming worry that come with the territory of being solely responsible for another person.

We are all just guessing our way, feeling our way – and without purpose and direction (aside from what we're brainwashed to think and do in our society) we falter, we stumble, and we criticise ourselves more than anyone else possibly can. We're programmed by our society to do that to ourselves. Think about all of the little wins you have achieved. Celebrate them! Congratulate yourself for every seemingly small and insignificant milestone.

Here's an example of a milestone: I made vegetarian bolognese and dished it up for my two fussy children tonight: because frankly I couldn't be stuffed making them a separate meal that would only end up on the floor. Wait for it… Both of my children ate their dinner! Not only was it different to their usual staple diet of dry crackers and cereal and anything 'not healthy' but it was full of goodness and meat-free. (Little celebration jig in my seat here as I celebrate like the dork that I am.)

So, if like me there are so many challenges in a day that it takes conscious effort to dig up the little wins, let's do this exercise to clear out some of the lower feelings that you are no-doubt harbouring daily.

Feeling wound up right now?

Take a deep breath. Calm down.

Take a moment to centre yourself with that spark inside, you know – You, the Soul.

Go there into your heart space and just be one with yourself a moment. Muster up all the stress, the worry, the frustration… all of the thoughts and feelings of guilt and helplessness. Gather it all up until it becomes a tangible 'thing' you could hold it in your hand. Feel it grow bigger as you feed all your lower, darker energies; the sour feelings and thoughts, judgements on self and others… Pull them all out of you and place them into this ever-growing ball of yucky stuff. **Now hand it over.**

Give it to God, to Source, to the Heavens, the Universe, the Angels (whatever resonates with you). Just hand it over. Give it away. How big was your ball of yucky stuff? See all of that came out of you, and you were carrying it around like a backpack of bricks. It has served its purpose, but you don't need to carry that baggage around with you every day. Carrying around all of this is going to hinder your ability to stay on mission, and your Precious one(s) need you to be at your best. Now, if you've successfully handed your lower energies over to higher planes for transmutation or dissolving – let's move ahead.

(If you need help, there are oodles of YouTube videos and channels you can investigate to release what no longer serves. I recommend you explore some options that resonate with you.)

*

We delved into 'The Soul' in Chapter Two – now shift your focus to your Precious one(s). Consider this… **They chose you, you are their chosen one.** Why do you think they chose you? I wonder if this Soul sat in the ethers flicking through a catalogue of potential parents, carers or partners and said, "Eeenie meeeenie minie MO! Yeah that'll do". Did they say, "She's got great legs, I'll take her" or "this guy looks like a barrel of laughs – I'll take him"?

Being the high frequency intelligent and honourable Soul that they are, those suggestions are hilariously unlikely. On a serious note, what would you consider to be your strengths? What lessons are you able to teach your Precious one(s) that no one else in the Universe could? Could you be their hero, teacher, advocate, leader, carer, healer and protector? Are you someone who will stimulate and challenge them? Are you someone that will enable them and allow challenging behaviour to become acceptable? Will you let society limit their potential by whacking the label on and expecting the professionals to take care of the rest?

Perhaps they chose you to help restore your faith, your love and expand your limited beliefs and mindset. Maybe they chose you to be of service to YOU and to heal YOU! Is it possible that you choose each other to repeat another life cycle together to achieve a greater purpose that was not yet accomplished in other life times? There are so many potentials – and it's all hypothetical at this point - but the aim here is to get your mind focussing on what your qualities are and what you can bring to this child/person's life. You have something special that this person/these people want and need for their Soul growth. When you start to look at it like this, how does your perspective shift? Do you see yourself in a new light now?

I often get down and out when I become cross with my children, and yep – I lose my cool and I raise my voice and have a bit of a tanty. Not my finest moments, sure. Parenting – it's hard work and occasionally we yell and scream, I'm not going to pretend I don't. (I'm real remember?) Some evenings when the children are finally in bed and I feel like I could crawl into bed for a thousand years or so – it starts. The process of 'shouldn't have done that'. Mummy Guilt enters the arena and she takes the stage.

I see my sweet little angels innocently sleeping and dreaming: the love that I feel for them wells up and occasionally comes out of my eyes and rolls down my cheeks. I wonder how I have been so mean, or not been able to maintain patience and composure like 'other parents' can. They deserve to have the best me that I can be, so why can't I just be the best *all the time*? Firstly, there's a fine line between telling children off and beating them up – I'm certainly not a horrible and abusive parent. But just this afternoon when I put the children to bed, it occurred to me that my children have chosen me – knowing that I would present these lessons in their lives.

Somehow my way of discipline and emotional coaching techniques and eventual exhaustion and frustration is teaching them something that they need to learn. Something they CHOSE to learn for their own Soul growth and expansion. **At times we get swept up in the frantic chaos of it all, and we forget what's important.** I'm sure we all do it. It's completely understandable! Between appointments for the Precious, any other Precious ones you care for and their needs, your own care needs, running a household, working or running a business, being a partner or slogging it out alone – no wonder we have days where just getting out of our PJs seems like a massive win!

I care about you, and your children. I want you to know that to be the best you can be for them – you have to 'show up' for yourself too. You must MAKE time to take care of you. I'm all for being selfless and being 'too busy' to care for myself – but it has taken me a while to realise that without me being on my A Game – shit falls apart. In the interest of helping you – right now – today, I will share something priceless that I have learned recently. Practice this yourself, in whatever way you feel connected to. What have you got to lose?

Mini Mum-Meditation

Recently I have learned a new way of meditating. I want to share it here, as I think you'll find it helpful. As nice of an idea it is to think I can meditate in peace and quiet for six hours a day, the reality is – I'm a mum. The rule of thumb seems to be that anytime a parent makes time to relax, the children sniff it out and make it their purpose to make certain that does not happen at any cost. (God love 'em! That ability for timely interruptions is like a super power!)

The more I made time to meditate – the more often I was interrupted. I altered the time I'd blocked in to meditate (yes, I have such a tight schedule that I needed to block it in). At night when the boys go to bed, I use that time work with Spirit or to study. It made sense to meditate before bed – only I miss the whole thing because I'm exhausted and pass out into a deep sleep.

I started to get up at 4am – surely that'll work. Yeah right. My Precious thought it was also a good time to wake for the day. It then became a routine for him to wake at 4am every morning. "Mum. MUUUUUM. Can I have the iPad? Can I have some breakfast? Is it still night? Where is my Spiderman toy? What's for dinner?" I tried it during My Little Precious' nap time. He'd wake up screaming. *Every. Single. Time.*

I know how much better I feel – and how much more patience I have when I have time to meditate, so it began to stress me out, that I couldn't find time to not stress out! Isn't that insane? Eventually, after I had been working with Source during some hectic moments, I remembered some tips I learned after reading a book written by one of my mentors (I highly recommend this book, "3 Seconds To Being Your Higher Self" By Arielle Hecht. I'm not an avid reader but this book resonated so deeply).

At the time I had been doing a lot of work with meditation and stripping everything back to zero point (where I am nothing but a pure spark, just a SOUL). I realised that during highly intense times of stress or chaos in my home (you feel me, it happens) I was 'zoning out.' *No, I don't mean I was dreaming of being on a deserted island with Tom Hardy, stay with me peeps!*

I focused on my Spark Within, the SOUL - until it pulsated like a warm flame in the centre of my forehead. I felt myself embodied in an ocean of love, with no physical body and no personality – just a beautiful spark. A beacon. A flame. Encompassing everything in my Soul history and yet nothing of this physical form that is my current skin suit. Pure bliss.

Aaaaah. That's nice.

As I did this more often in times of stress, I noticed how powerful the love of Source was, pouring golden light into my crown chakra… immediately. A warm and buzzing sensation washing over me and the frantic stress dissolved into peace and calm.

This zone-out place is where it's at. Without the bells and whistles and without the incense and special room and mood music – this was what I had been trying to achieve! All of this over-analysing and perfectionistic routine and it was always that simple. Simple, and yet the most powerful meditation – without the visions and Soul journey (which I absolutely love, but when you're spinning out and just need to chill – this is the way to go).

I call it a 'Mini Mum-Meditation'.

I have worked it down to a fine art, where I simply close my eyes for a brief few minutes, connect with my Spark Within and the Spark of Source. I receive a download of energy as it washes away any burdens or intense feelings – and resets me back to zero point.

From here, I find I can get on with it – big deep breath and off we go again with a renewed state of calm. I do this simple meditation at least five to ten times a day… and let me tell you – it is more powerful for me than sitting uncomfortably in a chair for an hour trying not to fall asleep.

Considering the Mini Mum-Mediation, I also started seeking out my children's Spark Within when they were having trouble with their own emotions. It is a new ritual that I find myself doing whenever I would usually feel the need to yell or carry on.

I look deep into their eyes and begin to feel for their Spark.

I ask them, "Where is your Spark? Can you feel your Spark? Feel my Spark. My Spark sends love to your Spark". Forehead to forehead, we connect. We share love. Sounds like something from a Disney movie but they respond to it, because they can feel it. This little ritual alone is usually enough to stop me in my tracks too and correct my own repetitive cycle… a cycle of conditioned parenting strategies that were used on me as a child.

Yelling and screaming – smacking and throwing things around, certainly worked to teach me when I was young! But I also learned extremely unhealthy habits to bring into my own children's lives, if I'm not careful. I'm aware of it, I am always challenging it and trying to 'un-learn' those behaviours. Negativity and hostility doesn't suit my children's sensitive energies, I suppose no child in the history of ever for that matter. The Spark connection technique I've recently adapted is far superior, far more loving and so much more rewarding and beautiful for everyone involved.

So, when tensions are high and in times of frustration (there are a few!) remember to focus on the light inside of them. Find their Spark and ask them to find yours (even telepathically). Connect the two spark's energies with intent, visualisation and focus. Feel the love. Send them *so much* love. In those weak moments where you think you are failing – or when that voice in your head says you "don't have it in you" or you "can't do this anymore"… remember this…

Your babies chose you.

Whether you understand it or not – you are giving them something they need. Sure, you'll make mistakes and you'll burn the candle at both ends and have 'bad days.' Move on from the bad days, tomorrow... you'll be better. It is important to remind yourself of what you learned from your own parents (the good and the bad) and that will curb your attitude toward your cherubs and impact your own parenting style. After all, you were that child on the receiving end of the harshness and discipline, are you content in making your babies feel the way you felt when you were powerless?

If in your heart of hearts, you truly believe you are in each other's lives for a divine purpose – this knowledge and awareness can hopefully give you back some of that power that you may often feel has been stripped away from you. **You've got this Mumma (or Daddy).** They knew that before they came here, **and that's why you're the Chosen One.**

Affirmation

I am Divinely Appointed this task.

I am qualified on a Soul level.

I have been chosen for this role.

I recognise The Soul Within others.

I too, am a Soul.

Affirmation

I am aware of the pure Divine light inside me

I am aware that I am pure love and light.

I bask in the Ocean of Love with the Creator

I receive blessings in a shower of golden light.

I give to Source my burdens, and I am uplifted and replenished.

I continue my journey with ease and grace.

Chapter Four

Mother's Intuition:
The bond between mother and child

This chapter is aimed at those mothers who may be reading. Even if you're not the mother of the person involved, please endeavour to continue through this section as it is all relevant somewhere along the line. No doubt you've heard the term 'mother's intuition' or 'mum knows best'. Until I became a mother myself, I really couldn't comprehend how true that statement really is. Think about a newborn baby who just cries. Mother can intuitively understand what her baby needs, or whether it is something to be concerned about or not. This does take some practice to decipher, because a baby crying is always sensitive for mum – because she feels her baby's pain… but she may not *know* how to help.

Let's think about young children who are yet to develop language and speech – as well as those people who are what is termed as 'non-verbal' or labelled with 'selective mutism'. During gestation the mother grows a tiny being within her womb. Her body is the living, breathing incubator for the nourishment and safety of the being and the environment for the foetus to thrive and develop. The unborn child and the mother literally have a bond, and through this physical connection - a metaphysical, energetic and emotional bond is maintained. While the mother quite literally breathes life into the foetus, she can often identify what the Soul is doing or feeling, or if there is a reason to be concerned.

I always thought of morning sickness more like motion sickness... every time my body adjusted itself to accommodate for the new resident, any slight movement from the foetus sent me into a vomiting, dizzy mess. Those days where bubs would do somersaults had me bedridden! With both of my pregnancies I suffered severe morning sickness, and aside from it being a medical phenomenon where pregnant women experience nausea and vomiting in their first trimester - I can also put it down to being an empath. I felt so deeply every little thing that was happening inside of my body. It took me almost six months with my second pregnancy to find my 'sea legs' and be able to keep food down.

Did you know that when the pregnant mother is unwell or feeling down – the foetus can transmit healing energy to the mother through their physical and metaphysical connection? This innate bond penetrates all reason and logic – and continues well after the child has entered the world and has become physically disconnected from the mother. I want to share with you an anecdote from my personal experience with my second child, Little Precious, who is not on The Spectrum.

I was about four months along with my second child when my life turned upside down. I was going through a marriage breakdown and the stress I was under whilst being pregnant began to affect my unborn child. One day I suffered a massive panic attack – my whole body convulsed uncontrollably, and I was screaming like a banshee. My legs gave way beneath me and I slumped to the stairs beneath me. I recall sitting on the front steps of my home sobbing and trembling, I couldn't breathe.

It wasn't long before I felt as though I was losing fluid and began having major abdominal cramps. It was as though I was going into labour… at sixteen weeks. I rushed myself off to the doctors – who sent me to the hospital. Being a small country town, the hospital said they didn't have the equipment to be able to give me an emergency scan. I just wanted to make sure my dear Little Precious was okay!

Three hours later, I finally made it into an ultrasound room in the next town - where the sonographer had to help me to calm down. Tears were streaming, and the uncontrollable shaking continued – as he began to run the test. The baby's heart rate was normal – and I felt so relieved that there even was a heartbeat.

(Because of course, although he wasn't born yet, I already loved this child with every fibre of my being.) The sonographer could see that I had experienced premature contractions. My unborn baby was feeling the state that I was in, and he wanted to come out now. I had dramatically altered his chemical and energetic environment and it was becoming unsafe for him.

A couple of months later, I was mid-separation and my dad was in the hospital having just been diagnosed with an aggressive Pancreatic Cancer. I was phoned by the sonographer saying that during my last scan they had forgotten to do one crucial measurement. Panic stricken I made the next available appointment and had to travel forty minutes to get another ultrasound. That drive was one of the longest of my life. Praise God, everything was fine with Little Precious... but I was a total mess. My life was a rollercoaster and my children (born and unborn) were the only things keeping me from losing my mind.

When the measurements were taken and Little Precious was perfect – I just cried with relief. When the sonographer took photos this time - what she captured was simply breathtaking, and I will remember it forever as one of the most profound and magical moments of my life. Little Precious pressed his hand up against the wall of my uterus at the most Divine and opportune moment. I heard a little voice say, "Calm down Mummy. "You're okay. I'm okay.

Just calm down Mumma". That day I rushed back to the hospital where my dad was still coming to terms with his cancer diagnosis – and I put the ultra sound photo beside his bed.

We both cried as we looked at it, and I told him what had happened. He saw it as a miracle, and he didn't even question me when I said, "I heard the baby talk to me, Dad! I swear I heard a little voice". Instead, filled with joyful tears – my dad said, "It's a God-send. Truly. Just magic. Isn't life just beautiful sometimes? One life is ending while another is beginning. Just magic".

I remember feeling guilty about what he said, it was heartbreaking. The way my dad said it was philosophically, wasn't spiteful or angry... just praying for another miracle – that he would get to meet this little angel. (He did, by the way. Dad stuck around until Little Precious was almost two. Little Precious was named after his Poppy, his given name meaning 'The Grace of God'.)

Just to confirm this story, my Little Precious is two and a half now. Most children have little catch phrases, things they love to say over and over. My Precious loved to say, "See you, hey!" when he was little. My Little Precious's favourite thing to say is "Are you okay? You're okay. You're okay. I'm okay. I'm alright". I know without a doubt now – that I most definitely heard Little Precious' voice that day. "You're okay. I'm okay. Just calm down Mumma."

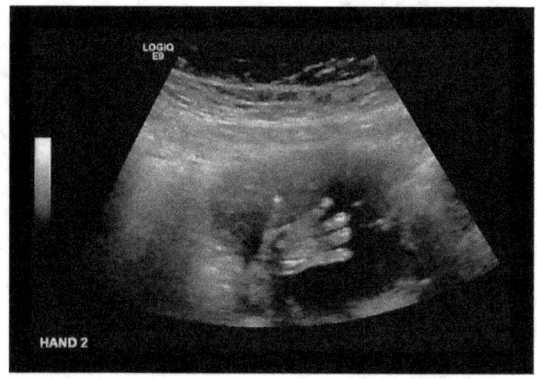

This bond, the unseen energy shared between them, is how the mother intuitively knows what her baby needs. She can tell the 'different' cries apart as there is a frequency, an energetic language between mother and child that only they can decipher. If your child is connected to you via the biological mother-child bond – this sensitivity is amplified, however not everyone chooses to accept or receive this bond. Some may reject or refuse it, and this is where Soul-contracts with other mother-figures take over.

A non-biological mother 'figure' can also pick up on this energy, as they have Soul contracts together in this lifetime. (This means that each Soul chose one another to fulfil certain roles in each other's lives.) Their energies can intertwine and allows a strong bond to be forged. Connection. Innate understanding. Unspoken knowingness. Isn't that magical? (For the dads reading this, mate – don't beat yourself up if your child only wants 'mum' when they are sad or unwell. It's an energy thing. You have your own zone too – but we'll get to that later!)

Have you ever had days where you were feeling particularly stressed or frazzled, depressed perhaps? Did you find the child (or children) seemed cranky, needy and 'out of sorts?' Whilst this appears to be a deliberate attempt to add to your bad day and ultimately creates more stress and frustration – there is another reason for it. **Your child is picking up on YOUR feelings, YOUR vibes.** Your child may feel how you feel. This may present as being cranky and emotional, perhaps expressing this with challenging behaviour. A new mother who is anxious about breastfeeding for the first time may become more stressed when baby refuses to latch. Babies can pick up that anxious vibe Mum's putting down, and as a result – mirror that back to her.

In this light, we may now begin to see a pattern of behaviour arise in our children. When the child is misbehaving or having emotional outbursts – focus on yourself for just a moment.

How are YOU feeling? What's on YOUR mind?

If you can shift your mind and energy toward feelings of love and peace, how do you think your child may behave? Test this theory. If nothing else, you'll get to a state where you can better handle your child's behaviour from a calm place, rather than a place of stress. You end up taking a good hard look at your own behaviour and feelings, and as such, take responsibility for shifting your perspective.

Children are sensitive to energy, vibration and frequency. It may sound silly but being mindful of our own energy and frequency can have a very profound effect on our children. It's not about blaming yourself for the child's behaviour – but simply realising that your energy output affects others. This is especially the case when we're talking about sensitive children, or high frequency Souls.

Excerpt from Unicorn Daydreams (Blog) - 23rd February 2018

'Sensitivity'

"…Finally – I had managed to get to bed before 10:30pm and was bright eyed and bushy tailed when my alarm went off at 5am (and by alarm, I mean eldest son shouting in my face that my alarm was too loud, and he couldn't watch his shows).

I did my new morning rituals and plugged in my headphones to do a guided meditation. STAY SITTING UP ANGELWING… Success – it was amazing, I felt fresh, I had visions and messages from new beings and wrote it all in my journal. I even had time to do some yoga-like stretching before little ninja woke up. That day – I felt amazing and full of beans all day, and finally achieved my goal of decluttering. (Yet again. How do we keep accumulating so much junk?)

As I was getting rid of all clutter or things that no longer serve us or haven't been used in ages; I could literally feel the liberation as I threw clothes into a pile that I knew I loved, but it was time to retire them to the bin or to goodwill. As I cleaned, I felt the stagnant energy shift – and my mood lifted with each accomplishment. It got me thinking of something my son said to me that morning. "It's your fault I am being naughty. I can feel your grumpy attitude and now I'm grumpy! You stop your being naughty then I will be a good boy. You need to let it go Mum, so I'm not grumpy."

At first, I was thinking, "Nice try, blaming me for your behaviour!" But I looked at him and I thought, "Oh yeah – you're super sensitive too". He was right. He was picking up on my underlying anxiety and grumpiness that things were piling up and we were all tripping over 1000 useless toys, and constantly reminded of haunting memories with Dad's funeral photos creating a shrine right in the living room. Dust everywhere – all of our allergies had flared up.

So, let's think about this. In this house we all have these sensitivities:

- Allergens: dust and hay fever type stuff
- Images: the memories they replay and vibrations they hold
- Physical items: again, with the memories and vibrations
- Each other's feelings and energy (and perhaps those of others not even dwelling here)
- Temperature. Too hot, no good. Too cold, no good.
- Food: One lactose intolerant, one healthy food refusal, I'm suddenly sensitive to meat and have inadvertently become a vegetarian.

It got me thinking – if our sensitivities are so heightened on such a small scale, imagine what the general unified consciousness is sensitive to…

I talk a lot about energy, because I'm an energy worker. But occasionally I need to take a break from other people's energy and just get a grip on my own and those closest to me. I find I am like a sponge – absorbing anything and everything and that creates a cloud around me that I work very hard to shift and balance.

It's obvious to me that my children are sensitive to my energy, which also carries vibrations of other's – and in turn I have been working diligently to clear it all up and be very particular with how I spend and attract energy...not just for my sake, you see? Our energy impacts others.

Now I put it to you, dear Soul. How sensitive are you right now? What aversions have you suddenly developed? It may be to a certain food, certain people, or certain thought patterns and habitual routines or addictions. How are they making you feel? What happens to you when you are sensitive to stuff?

The energies here are trying to work WITH us to initiate real positive change in our lives, and if we don't pay attention – it will work against us if we resist it. This resistance causes the symptoms and the pain associated with change. But if you really go deep and start to unpack the subconscious and subliminal messages your body and Soul harbours, you might find the willingness to do something different and get a different result. That result might just be your freedom and bliss."

– Angel Wing

When I refer to 'frequency' and 'energy' - think of it like a radio station (more on this in chapter 13). A clear channel sounds great! With a clear signal the message is relayed appropriately, and you can rock out to your favourite jams. How would your vibe shift if suddenly that station became muffled – with interference from talk-back radio? How would you feel if the awesome music you love so much was becoming static and crackling? What if there was no end to this static, if you had no power to turn it off completely?

Would it drive you insane? It would frustrate you, it would cause you to cover your ears and you'd sooner bash your head against a brick wall than continue listening to it. Your children, especially those high frequency children or people on The Spectrum – they not only pick up on your energy as interference and static…but they can feel it in their senses. It may cause their skin to crawl – and a simple touch may send them into sensory overload. It may make their ears sore – a loud or abrupt noise may send them spiralling into freak-out zone and they may cover their ears or need ear muffs to filter out the volume and high pitch sounds around them.

They may see things within their visual fields that others are blind to – see sounds, feelings, colours and interdimensional beings. This may cause them to 'stim' or flap their hands and move their fingers – as this is a way their physical body can regulate the sensory input they are receiving in this over stimulating manner. (More on Sensory Processing in chapter 8, but for now the focus is centred around you and your child.) Use that bond – feel it – send loving positive vibrations to your child. They need it more in times of distress and uncertainty. Focus on the connection you have and use it as a channel of communication – a private energetic chat room where you can telepathically and energetically level with your Precious in a language that you both innately understand.

What can you feel? What vibes are they sending you? There are hidden messages in this energy exchange that translate into words and thoughts, if you can just tap into them. Just like when they were little bubbas and you could differentiate which cry meant hungry and which one meant pain. It is important in this energetic connection that you are coming from a place of understanding and unconditional love. Use the Mini Mum-Meditation for a brief few moments to get yourself nice and centred.

From this heart space – you stand firm and loving, as a beautiful and unwavering anchor point for your Precious. Their energy needs a place to gravitate toward - to hold them in a safe space of love. Be the anchor that they know you are, that they chose you for. You have the power to understand your child like no one else, just like they understand you like no one else. After all, they are the only ones in the world who know what your heart sounds like from the inside.

Affirmation

I connect with my child with ease and grace.

I allow myself to feel their energy.

I easily understand vibrational language.

We are innately and spiritually connected.

I have the power to anchor their energy with my own state of peace and love.

I give thanks for this unique and beautiful bond.

Chapter Five

**Father-child bond
(and non-biological father connections)**

All families are different, and as such I was guided to separate some of the information I received from Spirit into different categories.

The biological and 'present' father.

When you become a parent, there's a lot of focus on the child and the mother. The role of the father and father figure is also very important, so I want to start off by saying to all the fathers out there – **I SEE YOU**. It's a tough gig. It's often a highly underrated, under-celebrated gig. But if you're doing it, you're doing the best you can – and whether they consciously show it or not – your family appreciates you for it.

Where you were once the unchallenged recipient of your partner's love and affection, you have had to take somewhat of the back foot in your relationship. It's no longer all about your relationship with your wife or life partner, but now you are ass deep in 'family man' zone. I know of a lot of blokes that have found the initial shock of this change intimidating, scary, and well – let's be honest, a bit of a shell shock. Some guys are excited, hands on and absolutely in their element with Dad life (finally an excuse for those awful dry jokes you've been telling for years).

Whatever you felt or continue to feel - was and is valid and real. But I wonder if anyone really asked you – how did you feel when you first became a dad? Do you have any support? Although at the beginning you may have felt invisible or left behind – your support and presence has not gone un-noticed I'm sure. I bet your wife/partner feels so blessed that she had you there to go through this journey beside her. Even if she doesn't show it, I bet it's in there somewhere.

You are potentially the Rock of the family – the stable foundation for your family as they rest their feet upon your shoulders. **You have just been promoted.** 'Key Support, Multi-tasking, Ninja-Warrior, (possibly sole Bread-winning) Extraordinaire!" (I just made that up on the spot, but I'm sure you could think of your own hilarious nickname!)

You may be the ear for your partner to vent to. You may be the sounding board for her to take her frustration and emotional outbursts out on. You may perhaps be the sole provider (even if for a short while after the birth of your child). You have immense pressure to match your partner's natural parenting style and somehow, you're expected to be nurturing and get in touch with your sensitive side… (and hey – that can be a challenge if you're not that way inclined.)

There are a lot of factors that contribute to a father's feelings after the birth of a child. In this space, often a man may feel he has no voice (or no right to one) and a rift may form between the father and the mother, or perhaps an unconscious tension or jealousy between the father and the child. It's not always the case of course, but all you have to do is look around you. Everything changes once you have kids, and it can put strain on a relationship especially if there are communication hurdles. (I often wonder whether my own marriage breakdown had something to do with this.) Some dads may be left feeling inadequate, pressured and a little left out. These situations, if they don't balance out or become noticed and validated, may stem into other more serious issues such as depression, anxiety, marital problems and a strained bond with the children.

On the other hand, some of you are just 'naturals' and can easily and confidently juggle family life with full time jobs and still be nurturing and loving dads. There is no need for comparison – for what you do in the position you are in is unique. I'm sure if you find yourself reading this, even if it's because your beautiful wife or partner handed it to you – you are kicking ass at this fathering thing. Kudos to you, no matter what your situation. Thank you, dads…for being the solid foundation. (Or for being vulnerable enough to share your feelings and be open with your partner, if you're that way inclined.) Thank you for your contribution to your family unit, even when you feel as though you're missing out on something or you're failing… you're doing your best and they love you for it.

Now although the mother of the child has essentially grown this little human inside of her own body – it was only possible with your integral contribution! Yup, there is a little child that was made from a piece of you, a little child who (on a Soul level) chose YOU to be their father. There are so many aspects of you that are melded into your Precious and we're about to delve a little deeper into recognising some areas that a father has a bond with their child like no other.

For a start, a Soul that has chosen another Soul to be responsible for them or to have a major role in their incarnation (human life) *instantly* recognises them. After all, if you chose something from a catalogue to serve a purpose for you, wouldn't you know it when you saw it? Wouldn't you recognise it if it arrived on your doorstep amid other random items? **Your child, the Soul – connects with you just by being near.** Through your eye contact. Through your energy. Through the sound of your voice that plays a familiar song to them in a frequency they cannot deny. Through the gentle rhythm of your heartbeat.

Although a father may feel stressed and nervous, their child seeks comfort from the stability and underlying love that they sense from dad – even if he doesn't feel it within himself. Quite often children see the beauty in us we don't see in ourselves. It's one of the most profound things about being a parent, someone loves you – not for what you can do for them – but just because you are you. Think back to the infant stages... The child felt you, he who's energy wasn't harshly impacted by post-partum hormones and mental exhaustion to the same degree as a new mum. Sometimes, dad's energy is a nice chilled out break from mum who is constantly pressuring herself and who's body is recovering from the massive adjustments of childbirth, breastfeeding and motherhood.

Did you feel that? When you held your baby in your arms? Did you see that they looked at you like they were 'home' or that they calmed down and fell asleep on your chest? I bet if you think back, you can dig up at least one occasion where you were the hero one sleepless night and managed to get the baby to stop crying just like magic.

As your child/children grow you will come to learn the traits and characteristics they possess that will make you laugh (or cry) because they're just like you in those unique ways. Your gifts and knack for certain hobbies or interests may be obvious traits in your child as well. It's likely they will do it harder and faster than you ever did, because they're their own unique version of you... They're pieces of you, the newer, more hardcore model!

With pieces of their parents and the information they bring in from previous lifetimes - they're pretty spectacular. They embody a much higher frequency than their parents, just as we came in at a higher vibration than our parents. Through these examples: eye contact, energy, voice frequency and tone, similarities in personality or interests – you may be able to shine the light on some bonds that you already have with your child. You may be able to concentrate on each example and hone in on them to re-establish or deeply improve your connection with your Precious.

If you are a father who feels they have a strained bond with their child, or have trouble connecting with them - refer to chapters 2 and 3. Connecting with the Divine Spark within yourself and within your child is always a great way to truly 'see' them, and to interact from that space of unconditional love and peace. If your child is sensitive to sounds and vibrations, try quietening your voice a little when you speak to them. How do they react? If your older child on The Spectrum has difficulty understanding humour and sarcasm, try keeping your words factual and focus on something that you know makes them laugh. (It may be wise to avoid jokes with complicated or 'dry' undertones.)

My Precious isn't exactly the sporty, 'kick-the-footy-with-dad' type. Rather than try to force Precious to do something that he enjoyed as a child, Precious' dad spends quality father-son time doing something that he knows his son loves. They occasionally make videos with the iPad as though My Precious is giving a 'Toy Review' on YouTube. It is a special interest - and although tedious at times, it's super adorable – and he loves it.

Our boy prefers this interaction over being forced to run around playing ball sports – which he finds challenging and frustrating, both physically and mentally. This experience improves the innate bond they already have and creates new pathways to connection and adoration between them. It provides more opportunity for conversation, and the excitement of planning for future interactions (because it was so much fun, he'll want to do it again and again!)

That's parenting, right? Doing the shit that they love even if it's tedious to you. I've seen and heard about dads that dress up in tutus and have tea parties with their daughters – and mothers that dress as batman and cosplay with their kids. It's a bit more complicated here, if you have a Precious on The Spectrum, but it doesn't have to be. Dig deep, find the patience and the creativity to come up with something unique, playful and meaningful – just for the two of you. It'll be the most fun you'll have had in ages!

Lack of presence from a biological father or biological mother (Single parents and adopted or foster parents).

So, what about the children who grow up without a biological father or mother? For one reason or other, not all biological parents are present, or active 'mums' and 'dads' in their children's lives. Many sole parents may harbour feelings of guilt, anger and resentment in their child's defence. There may be feelings of lack, pity, blame, burden – although mostly subconscious, it's still there.

What if I told you that this child *chose* this circumstance for their Soul evolution and growth before they came here? It sounds silly, right? Why would you choose to be without one or both of your parents? Why would you choose to grow up in a 'broken home'?

Because this Soul needs to experience this type of hardship, to experience the opportunities and the lessons. They may learn to be self-sufficient, to discover themselves without being in someone else's 'shadow' or 'footsteps' so to speak. It will be a blessing for them, if *they* chose to see it this way. If you *encourage* them to see it this way. This child (or children) will learn how it feels to be the child without a dad (or mum) – and this in turn has the potential to make them a fantastic, attentive and dedicated father or mother in later life – should they take that path.

They will value the parental figures they do have – and although it won't always be easy, the evolution of their Soul will be expansive.

They could also learn love and respect for women, as they'll see how hard their mum tries to be everything they need (to compensate for their lack of paternal influence). They could learn how to be strong and independent without the need for a 'text book' family. The circumstances could offer them a choice to either repeat or break a repetitive cycle, and that is their journey. You can't walk that for them. There's a lot to do with perception and influence as well. If you're constantly complaining about their biological parent or wishing ill upon the other, your Precious will likely grow up with the same opinion. This is energetically toxic stuff, so it is important to deal with that stuff internally and clear out as much as you can of your own pent up emotion.

Being the mum and the dad at the same time is a super-task. I have so much love for you! Even part-time sole parenting is hard. Where others have their partners to chip in and help out, you may fall short of a spare pair of hands. You seem to find a way to grow a third arm – or if you're anything like me – tend to use your voice as a motivator when you've got your hands full. We absolutely adore and love our amazing kiddies – but there's no denying it can be exhausting and extremely testing.

I know you're exhausted and some days you don't think you can do it any longer – but I assure you, you've got this. You're the only one who *can* do what you do, and your children are going to grow up to be wonderful, amazing and well-adjusted adults because they have you. **If this is you, you're doing an amazing job Mumma/Daddy!** You are all they need right now. But please, please take care of yourself. You're no good to them if you're burned out. Nourish your Soul and spirit, not just your body. It'll create more ease and grace, believe me.

Parents with Autism.

As we go through these different types of connections and bonds, Spirit has encouraged me to connect with those parents who may also be on the Autism Spectrum, or who suspect they may be. It is common that after a child's diagnosis, a parent will find the similarities within the fields of assessment and this may cause them to reflect about their own undiagnosed challenges or seek advice about their own behaviours or triggers. For parents who are also on The Spectrum, as you're aware – nothing in your life is black and white, and there may be some things in this book that are accurate for you and some that you cannot relate to at all.

That's completely okay, and there's no 'one size fits all'. Connecting with your child may be a little more complicated for you, as you too have your own social and emotional blockages, boundaries and preferences. If you are ever concerned that you have less ability to connect with your child, let me reassure you that you have a perspective into your child that others do not. The way you see the world and experience it, gives you a deeper understanding to the world through the eyes of your child/children. You have a leg-up when it comes to trying to understand or perceive the view from their energetic disposition, because you are both on the same wave length (or very similar).

This is a prime space for connection and understanding between you and your child – and this is an energetic flow. Within this energetic flow, there is no need for words, so long as the intention is loving and pure. If you have difficulty expressing emotion or physical affection in a 'mainstream' way – please don't be hard on yourself. Chances are that is just how your Precious likes it too. You have a love language just like everyone else, and once you figure out what that is and how you express your deep emotional stuff, you will realise that you are not lacking anything, nor is your child missing out on anything from you.

Your energy exchange is extra-important. Your words, kindness, acceptance, understanding and empathic energy are supportive and loving – this is sufficient, this is YOUR normal. Just because other people do things differently or express love in other ways, that doesn't mean you are incapable or cold. It means your love has a different dimension to it – and that is simply beautiful. Spirit discusses with me often, that attention needs to be given to situations where one or both parents have Autism. In some circumstances this can relate to aggressive outbursts and obsessive-compulsive tendencies and habits. Particularly the 'undesired behaviours', especially if similar traits are already present in your child.

The reason for this attention is because there may be such similarities that it begins to create a polarity in the relationship. That is to say, you may be so similar that you butt heads - a clash of the similarities and the standoff of strong wills. Once attention is drawn to such things, it can be a fun way to work together. This may include emotional coaching or sensory activities, similar interests and skill building in a mutual setting.

You could find a trigger that you both have in common – and push through it together. (i.e. You both find it a trigger to be in a busy supermarket with all of the sensory input. Make a plan and go together, be there for one another. When you get home, discuss what you felt, how your body reacted and right there – you will find that zing that helps you to connect on a profound, understanding and empathetic level.)

Something else creative (and less stressful) could be - if your Precious loves analysing movie scenes frame by frame, repeating the same movies and so forth (and you consider yourself a bit of a movie buff) you could make a game or a video blog about specific themes and repetitive icons. I mean, have you seen some of the random stuff on YouTube that our kids are watching? Who would have thought a child watching another child opening a thousand Kinder Surprise Eggs would be so entertaining? There's a niche for everything!

Get creative and use it to connect with your Precious! As it would take me numerous chapters and insurmountable time and effort to try to cover every unique parenting situation – hopefully this gives a general enough view about connection to begin with.

To recap: we have established a few golden ways to connect, reconnect, and maintain connection with your Precious, and the importance of reflecting on your own self and coming from a place of unconditional love and peace when doing so. There's no doubt you're loving your Precious Ones with every inch of your being. It's only going to help your child (or children) if you make a conscious decision to be aware of your energetic frequency – your headspace… and always act and speak from a place of love, integrity and Soul-connection.

Connection is the starting point for empathy, learning, accepting, and overall being in a firm position to help anchor and support your child - from a heart space and not an intellectual or obligational one.

Affirmation

My bond with my child is strong and unique.

My role in my child's life is important and Divine.

My child benefits from my love.

My child's love moves me.

I give thanks for my beautiful bond with my child.

I interact with my child from a heart space of unconditional love

I am a loving anchor for my child's high energy.

Chapter Six

Integrity, Time, Patience, Respect.

There are times in our lives where we come across people whom (for whatever reason) we don't trust. It may be their demeanour, their reputation, their words and actions or just the feeling of distrust and dishonour that we pick up energetically from them. Sometimes you can pin-point exactly what it is, and other times you just feel it in your gut. Spidey senses start tingling. You know, the heebie-jeebies. What is happening here, is we are discerning someone's integrity. Whether you consider yourself intuitive or not – this is the utilisation of your innate intuitive nature. (Welcome to recognising one of your superpowers!)

A person on The Spectrum has a super-sensitive integrity meter. As they hold a naturally high vibration, a person on The Spectrum has an inner lie-detector. This also contributes to the part of them that finds it uncomfortable or impossible to sugar coat things or to lie. This inner 'gauge' impacts whether they are willing to give a person their attention, eye contact, energy or time.

Here is an anecdote from my experience with a child that was not my own, (a child that I will always remember; who taught me more in half an hour than ten books could have).

The child who couldn't speak.

I indirectly knew a child who was classified at the time as 'non-verbal'. I will refer to them as *Casey. This child was referred to as if they couldn't understand, they didn't comprehend the spoken word. I was told things like this – in front of the child. In a few encounters I had already heard people saying, "Casey doesn't get it, hasn't got a clue" or "Casey can't talk, Casey's Autistic, they don't understand". It was as though Casey wasn't part of the world, just *in* it.

I felt empathy for the child, and the family. I felt bad because my son appeared to be on the high functioning end of the scale, and from all accounts this child had higher special care needs. I was interested to have an interaction with this child and see if I could make a connection. The child wasn't familiar with me in any way, and as we walked together I watched on as the chaperone became frustrated with the constant interruption as the child wanted to sit and play in the dirt.

We'd be walking along and suddenly Casey would run in the opposite direction. The child continued to wrestle against the chaperone and was essentially being dragged along. (We've all done this at one point or other with our stubborn children, so I didn't think it out of the ordinary.) We got to a clearing and again, Casey melted away from us to sit down in the dirt. I sat down beside the child. I began to talk about the dirt, even though they made no eye contact with me or gave any social cues to indicate they understood or cared what I was saying.

I continued to say, "Dirty. Yucky! Grass. Weeeeee! Grass in the air. I like the grass. Do you like the grass and the dirt?" Still, the child stared off into space with a blank stare and a smile - as if what they saw was so much more amazing than what I could see. Casey wasn't playing ball and began to run away again. Instead of chasing, I ran beside the child as if it were a race. I stopped abruptly and yelled "STOP!" *Casey kept running. "Aaaaand GO!" I yelled and over-dramatised the running again. I did this a few times repetitively. I was playing an awesome fun game and I was playing it by myself – alongside the child.

Then…

I yelled "STOP…" Casey stopped.

There was no eye contact - Casey didn't turn around to face me - but I could see from the body language and the tilted head toward my direction, that my game was understood. I couldn't believe it. I yelled "Hooray! Good job!" and clapped and cheered. The chaperone asked me, "How did you do that? How did you get Casey to stop?" My response was, "I didn't do anything. I'm just playing".

We continued the game for a few more paces and as a bit of a 'hugger' I thought I'd see if Casey would let me pick them up. I asked for a hug and although Casey's face was turned away, the body language engaged me with arms open. Almost momentarily Casey squirmed to get down, so I began to play the running game with the child in my arms.

"Ready... Set... Go," I said, and then ran like a galloping horse a few paces. "Stop." I repeated the words with the actions, (a sensory activity relating to speech that I had recently learned). "Ready. Set..." I waited and looked at Casey eagerly with a big open mouth grin. Although they still weren't making eye contact with me, Casey said it. **Casey said the word "GO!"** I had to hold back tears. This child who 'never spoke' (or likely had limited vocalised words) just said "go". Within half an hour, Casey had said 'go', 'stop', 'again', and 'car'. By the end of the hour, the child was holding my hand and had made eye contact with me and even smiled at me.

I will always remember that day, because although my own child had less severe 'symptoms' of Autism than Casey – I learned so much from that interaction. I took that new information home and practiced it with my own son. I often think about that day when my own sons refuse to speak, or to listen, or display challenging behaviour. I've even used it with my Little Precious, my niece and other children when I think it's appropriate.

Why was this interaction so meaningful? Well, that little Soul touched my heart that day… and I'm pretty sure I touched theirs too. I showed them my integrity. I treated the child like the four-year-old that they were, an innocent and intelligent little being, a SOUL. I used sensory input based on what I could clearly see they liked, to encourage the words to fall out naturally, as if by accident.

*

If I have been criticising my son, whether to his face, behind his back or even in my head – he feels it, he hears it, he bloody-well knows! We don't like to admit it, or perhaps we're not even consciously aware of it – but we hold little grudges, or we get shitty over the things that our children do (or don't do) that frustrate us. Even if we don't voice it, we hold the thought and energy – and they know, they feel it.

If my Precious clams up or he acts out, it may be because my own integrity is skewed. I must check in with myself... a lot. It's not always the case, especially now that he's developed an attitude and knows how to get his own way – but I do have to constantly think about what vibes I'm putting out.

I ask myself a few basic questions. You can try this too.

1) Am I restricting his ability by using the words 'can't' and 'won't' – 'bad' or 'naughty'?
2) Am I feeling angry or disappointed with him?
3) Do I have unrealistic expectations of him?
4) Am I comparing him to other 'typically developing children'?
5) Is the fact that I need to put in so much extra effort (sometimes with little to no result) creating unintentional feelings of resentment or hostility toward him?
6) Am I letting my personal problems and feelings overwhelm me and tarnish my Zen?
7) Have I given him enough attention, I mean – proper, undivided listening and quality interaction?

Often, admittedly... I have been doing any number of those things unintentionally. Generally – just the act of focusing attention onto those possibilities is enough to make you realise that sometimes they are not the issue... *we are.* Once we begin to debunk the energetic and emotional underlying stuff that's going on, we can dissolve the stuff, we admit to it by thinking about it. We can shift the energy back to a place of unconditional love, because deep down – the last thing we want to do is make our Precious ones feel awful, unaccepted, limited or downtrodden.

Back to integrity...

The truth is, and here it is – no matter where their name sits on the Autism Spectrum, they CAN understand, maybe not what you *say* necessarily, but how your energy feels to them. How the individual receives the input around them is unique to the Soul – which is why there can be no one way to describe or understand Autism. I believe, a Soul on The Spectrum can hear you and understand you, maybe just not in the conventional way that *you* understand others. Their language? Their speech? It's all in there.

Their awareness and perceptions are so much 'different' to what society is used to (hence the diagnosis in the first place) but that doesn't mean to say it's not there. The trick is to find out what 'energetic language' your Precious uses, their sensory preferences, their ABILITIES not their 'disabilities.'

I work with Spirit when it comes to matters of speech – as I am interested in why a Soul may not be able to speak. Spirit corrects me… that if a Soul 'cannot' speak, they have chosen not to be verbal in this lifetime for their Soul growth and evolution. Where there is lack of speech, there may be an intense super-powered sense to replace it… (we'll cover that later).

In others who don't speak; with no medical, physiological reasoning behind the lack of speech - it's like a muscle that hasn't needed to be used in previous lifetimes. Within dimensions of extremely high frequency, communication is telepathic and energetic. Speech is not something that is required.

Since incarnating here into this density and restriction – speech and verbal language is often a learned skill for these high vibe Souls. Like a muscle that needs some training and some stretching – some encouragement and some sensory and mentally -stimulating motivation.

It's all well and good to understand or feel that being non-verbal was this Precious one's choice or that it makes them better at a different skill – but that doesn't make it easy on you, the parent/caregiver. I am a firm believer in trying, and let's face it – in this society, speech makes things much easier. We are beings that need to communicate – we long for connection. We long to be validated, seen and heard.

Just a few tips for your journey to encouraging and supporting the development of speech and other forms of communication with your Precious (including emotional regulation and coaching) …

Make sure you have INTEGRITY, because they'll sense it if you don't.

Find your centre, connect with your own inner peace and work from the heart space. Spend the TIME to really try to interact and connect with your Precious in a way that THEY comprehend and enjoy. Sometimes we're such slaves to the clock that we forget what's truly important. It's not the money you spend or the fancy stuff you give them – it's that thing, which - once it's passed, you can't get it back…

Make Time.

A little extra time can make the world of difference, that's a great way to show your love (especially if that's an area you may struggle with expressing). It may seem all for nought in the moment – but all is not lost. Keep doing what you're doing. You can never spend too much time interacting and loving, teaching and learning with your Precious.

Patience and Perseverance.

(Your Precious may learn at their own pace, delayed in their speech and movement – so I'm sure you're an expert at patience already!) I often feel disheartened and like an epic failure if I try a new activity with my Precious and he doesn't respond or reciprocate the interaction the way that I hoped…the way other children seem to. It's never a judgement on my Precious, but the pressure I put on myself that I am somehow doing it wrong can be… well, a bit depressing.

This still happens – just today I sat with both of my children to do a table top activity using stickers and coloured sand. Little Precious (2 years old) was like a miniature mad scientist, hypothesising how fast he could destroy and deconstruct everything on the table... My Precious (6 years old) was enthralled for about five minutes, we had some beautiful interactions… and then I lost his attention to a lengthy Minecraft rant, resulting in "all finished now" and a quick escape. I ended up doing the activity on my own, and dammit – my sand art was fabulous! (Is it sad that I enjoyed it?)

For my Precious, his inability to focus for extended periods has improved so much since starting Primary School, but it was especially challenging in the early years. I could only keep his attention for three seconds – to a maximum of two minutes.

I tried and tried again, the same thing – repetition, repetition and more repetition. Ground Hog Day style repetition. I won't lie, it was exhausting, at times frustrating and upsetting, but eventually I could see that it was paying off in amazing ways, and still to this day, I see the results.

(This kid has an astounding memory. Randomly he can recall an activity we did from back when he was two or three. "I did the playdough and we cutted the straws with the funny scissors when I was a baby." He could even tell me where we were, what was on the TV in the background and any other random insignificant trivia… as if he were right back there now. All my effort, he took it in, even though it appeared that he wasn't even really 'there' at the time.)

*

Most importantly…RESPECT.

Respect your child and their rights to feel and experience the world in the way that comes naturally to them. An example of respect in my family – is that when my Precious experiences happiness, excitement and joy – he stims, or self stimulates. What this looks like for him is he flaps his hands profusely, shakes his legs or bounces, pulls faces amid contagious smiles and laughter. I often hear people say, "Oh nice dancing!" (I giggle to myself because he's not dancing, this is just how he expresses his happiness emotion. It's bloody adorable.)

I inherited a saying that I saw on Google, and I use it still to this day. **"He's flappy cos he's happy. Deal with it."** I love seeing him stim, because that's his way of showing his feelings, his bliss. The more he stims the happier he is – so if he's not flapping and flicking his fingers as he speaks or rocking and jumping up and down in his chair - then that indicates he's not so happy.

I respect his feelings and his sensory processes. I work my ass off to learn about his sensory needs, how _he_ specifically regulates and what he requires help with _to_ regulate. If there's nothing else you do to understand or help your child – this fine tuning, Soul-specific learning is the crucial thing you should do. It's **so** important.

Brutal Honesty. No sugar coating.

Depending on your Precious, you may or may not find this helpful – but I have learned the hard way;

a) Be clear: subtle undertones are misunderstood or missed completely.

b) Be specific and brief: words and instructions can be taken *very* literally.

c) Be honest: there ain't no lying to my boy – ever.

In this light, Precious and I have a very honest and brutal dynamic when it comes to how we speak to each other. If I want him to pick up his dirty socks, there's no point me saying, "Excuse me mate, would you mind picking up your socks pretty please, baby, darling, Shnookums?" He'd likely respond with "I do mind, actually. No thanks. You can do it, baby, darling, Shnookums".

Instead I'd have to say, "You need to pick up the socks and put them in the laundry room right this second please, because if I need to pick them up it will be frustrating, and I will get cross".

I often have discussions with my Precious to apologise – I've gotta' get real with him. I am human, and I have bad days (and yes, I'm known to drop the F bomb) and I need to explain *why*. I level with him, I explain that I sometimes I get flustered and busy and that I shouldn't get cross – but hey – we all have our moments.

I might say, "I was a bit sad, I was feeling like I was having a bad day. That is not your fault, and I shouldn't have said that". I also explain what he did that earned my reaction. We analyse it together. I give him alternatives – "Instead of talking over the top of me and barking orders (while I'm elbow deep in the dishes, talking to a distressed relative on the phone, with a toddler hanging off my leg) – it would be RESPECTFUL to wait patiently."

I respect him enough to be honest with him, even if it means being a bit too honest. That's how he rolls, that's the language he understands, and I give it to him straight. He gives it to me straight too, and then some! But whilst there are boundaries, rules and a superiority chart, mutual respect goes a very long way.

Side track for a moment – but this may also be helpful

Respect is so important to me, and not something my Precious understands in black and white. Currently, it's one of his biggest hurdles. After much deliberation and many screaming fits and oppositional defiance episodes... I have designed a reward chart to reflect what 'respect' means, and some very practical lessons to teach him in his daily life.

1) We have a set of rules, (Dos and Don'ts). On one side - all the things he can do that are respectful is listed: i.e. helping around the house, using nice voices and nice manners,

playing gently with others, doing as instructed, self-care rituals etc.

Don'ts: yelling at people, hurting others, using mean words and angry voices, not taking care of his teeth and other self-care needs etc.

2) I designed three separate categories of 'Respect Tickets' that he can earn. Once they're earned they cannot be removed (positive reinforcement).
   a) Respect for Others
   b) Respect for Myself
   c) Respect for my Home.
3) Precious needs to earn at least five tickets a day to get to use the iPad or PlayStation.
4) Bonus tickets (more than 5) go onto a separate chart with a bigger goal (the latest is an Xbox. *He really wants that one.* The cost – 20 bonus tickets in two months... or no dice.)

As a visual learner – he needs clear rules, tickets and charts physically and colourfully placed in front of him, so he can organise the information in his mind. No tickets = No iPad. No PlayStation. No treats. Easy. **There's no wiggle room. Clear. Simple. Repetitive. Interactive. Fun.** So far, it's making a huge difference in his behaviour. Instead of a three-hour standoff; I remain calm and say, "You know you need to do this to earn your tickets, because it's respecting yourself. I don't think you're going to get your X-box by your birthday. Isn't that a shame?"

He's very clever, so of course once he gets what he is aiming for, he'll likely not be so responsive – and then it will be time to change it up a bit and set up a new system.

It's tedious, time consuming, and I'll be honest - sometimes I just can't be bothered. But as mentioned above – patience and repetition, repetition! We're all teachers and students – all at the same time. There's a fine balance between picking your battles, and letting your own rules get too far gone that Precious has outsmarted your system and taken advantage of your weakness!

We are learning every day. We are teaching every day. We can't afford to get too hung up on yesterday's mishaps – tomorrow it'll be better. Re-centre. Breathe. Remember, all of this is part of the bigger picture. One day your child will look back at these years and be so grateful that you did what you did, and so will you.

Affirmation

I interact with my child with Integrity.

I treat my child with respect and honour his or her unique perspective of their world.

I make time to see the world through my child's eyes.

My connection to my child grows with love and understanding every day.

I allow patience to wash over me.

My life is full of blessings and opportunities for growth.

I give thanks for my magical life.

Chapter Seven

Therapists, Courses and You (Oh My!)

As a parent or person who is involved with the Autism World, you are now already familiar with at least a few therapy services that benefit your Precious Ones. We are fortunate that there has been many years of research and studies on the physical, physiological, psychological and educational needs of someone on The Spectrum – thus the wide range of resources, education, equipment and therapies we now have at our fingertips.

Unless you're in a country that has funding for such therapies – and even before diagnosis - this can be extremely costly and time-consuming. It's intimidating at first and can be completely overwhelming! Your head may be spinning with the influx of information that you're given - the professionals tell you what they think is going on and ask what seem to be the most random and bizarre questions... It's as though you need to watch your child with a magnifying glass every second of the day and see them through the eyes of a trained Occupational Therapist just to fill out a checklist.

It does become easier, I promise. You learn to shift your focus, you start to look out for certain types of behaviours, triggers and patterns. You focus on what your child strongly likes and dislikes. You develop a lens for it, so to speak. Soon enough you view your Precious through a kaleidoscope of information and input that leads to a deeper understanding. It can be hard, for sure… but also magical.

Perhaps you have learned by now that the more you – the lover of this Precious – get involved and learn the ways of the therapists; the more empowered you are on a daily basis to actually help them in meaningful and ground-breaking ways. It is most likely *you* who spends the most time with them. It is most likely *you* who sees them at their best and their worst. It is most likely *you* that is walking around like a zombie with the weight of the world on your shoulders. It is most likely you that is waking up every day, wondering how you're going to get through it all again with your patience and sanity intact.

I know it's overwhelming, and at times, seems all too hard. But you **can** do this. You're already doing it. It's like anything you do consecutively – it becomes natural and normal after repetition. This parenting gig is not without its testing and exhausting moments, that much is universal. For you, things may be more complex – but it's your normal now.

I'll say it again, though – it can also be magical!

Integrating therapeutic activities and routines into their everyday life is a sure-fire way to create positive change. This streamlined, Soul-specific, tailor made routine, becomes a container of sensory-supported understanding and creates more opportunities for breakthroughs and milestones. It's allowing your Precious to play a game *they can win*, with just a few tweaks. Although I have a very Spiritual point of view and the methods I use in my home are somewhat 'kooky' perhaps - I am a huge advocate for therapies such as Speech Pathology, Occupational Therapy, Physiotherapy, Social Skills-Building Playgroups, Psychology and so on.

I have seen such interventions make a huge difference in my child's development and successes. I have practiced and implemented what I have learned merely as a bystander, as a witness – and I have seen instant results.

One might consider me a rookie, I mean, I've only been living in the Autism World for just under seven years... however, I take everything seriously and think about it deeply. I'll admit, at first, I grappled with dark internal stuff that came up for me. My parenting strategies were (and still are) constantly under surveillance and scrutiny. It wasn't a nice feeling and created a lot of anxiety for me to be 'the perfect mum'. This was unnecessary pressure, unfair pressure - and I did it to myself.

Once I stopped being defensive and feeling accused of 'not doing it right' or feeling constantly judged and assessed by the professionals supporting my Precious – and began to work WITH them... there was a giant shift. It's okay not to be perfect. It's okay to have 'human' moments. It's okay to admit it, too. The path of least resistance is to stop feeling like a failure and getting stuck in the zone of feeling criticised and victimised – and start being a team player. That is the only way you're going to be able to make waves of differences for your Precious – and you can't do it all alone... not without burning the candle at both ends and being useless to help anyone.

Becoming a team player has uncovered a new aspect of myself too, that I didn't know was there. I have become passionate and enthralled. I believe we can make a huge difference to these kids, and to this planet's entire future (because our children ARE the future). **The path we're on together my friends... is the Hero's Journey. It's no small thing, and it involves being teachable, and being WILLING to do the work. But that's why you're here... you hear the call too.**

What I've learned so far, not as a medical professional but 'just' as a parent – I have seen work on any child I interact with, not just those on The Spectrum. All children are wonderful, pure, divine, and sensitive beings. I've practiced speech therapy techniques, emotional coaching and 'sensory diet' activities with my youngest child, my young family members and friend's children.

I'm not the child whisperer (honestly, some kids run a mile when they see me because I like cuddles and I talk a lot!) but I couldn't count how many times a parent or carer has looked at me bewildered and asked, "How did you *do* that?" Whether they have watched me diffuse my own child's heightened behaviour or perhaps their own, I don't realise I have even done anything. All I tried to do was to see the SOUL – and figure out why they are having such a hard time in the moment and help them out of it. Or to help the parent who looks so exhausted and embarrassed – (we've all been there) and help them out. You might be surprised how many people have a knack for it, you probably do too!

Education. Everything and everyone provides a learning opportunity. You may call me a bit of a dork (and I totally am) but I'm also just someone who likes to know how things work. If there's a way I can help someone, or to make someone's life better – I will. If I can find a way to help my baby, to help children in general – I will search, and I will learn. I would (and still do) attend my child's therapies with the intention to absorb as much information as possible. Just by observing action and reaction, you can pick up the subtlest cues that might lead to the most enormous breakthroughs.

Being brutally honest with the therapist, and with yourself, deepens the ability for the them to use their credentials to provide meaningful and practical support – with knowledge and tools we have no idea about. They can't truly know the scope of your issues and challenges until they see it, or until you share it. I ask loads of questions about the purpose of certain exercises, what they're aiming to achieve and how I can help. I ask if there are certain things I should or shouldn't say and gain the validation a lot of the time that what I am doing is already awesome. (Sometimes, that's the most valuable part.)

I am constantly building up extra 'tools for the toolkit' so to speak. I am always churning ideas to incorporate new strategies into our daily routines. (Kids will be kids – eventually they catch on to what you're doing... and the whole exercise flops. It's best to stay one step ahead!)

Anecdote.

In the early days it seemed like many of the therapist's activities or terminology would aggravate or distress my Precious. With a combination of energy reading and knowing my child's warning signs – it wasn't long before I began to speak out. The often shy and nervous 'me' had suddenly taken a back step, and Mumma Bear stepped forward. (Not the grizzly kind; more the gentle, peace-loving hippie kind of bear.)

I had to. He couldn't speak for himself, and I was/am his advocate and his voice.

For me, it wasn't just about rocking up to the session and sitting back while someone else did the dirty work *for* me. It wasn't about only 'working' on it an hour a week and then expecting different results. Visual Schedules were something that we were using at home, for My Precious had very limited speech and visual sensory preferences. We arrived to Occupational Therapy one day, where there were several cue cards lined up in a row on the wall. This was the Visual Schedule for the session, made up with each card representing an activity.

My Precious began to punch the wall, yell and scream, throw toys around and refused to focus on the schedule. He tried to escape the room, running out into the hall, and was basically just in complete refusal of cooperating with any instruction at all. I realised that seeing everything all in one place - lined up together was overwhelming for him. As I struggled with him in my arms, physically punching and kicking me, I suggested to the therapist that **one** item at a time might work better.

I suggested that when one activity was completed we place the cue card in the 'Finished Box' and *then* move on to the next one. (We had a 'finished bag' at home – made by my sister from checkered material. It was used to transition him from one toy or activity to the next. It also helped when we wanted him to give up something he really wanted to keep playing with. It helped him with the concept of time, as well.)

The therapist looked puzzled, because let's be honest – she had the experience and text-book knowledge. That wasn't the way it was supposed to be done. But at that moment, she smiled with relief that I had some insight and said, "Thank you for telling me, that's extremely helpful. We'll give that a shot". **It worked immediately.** When only one task card was on the board, he stopped and focused on what it was. Oh, yes – shaving foam, he liked that activity. Suddenly, he participated willingly, knowing what was displayed was the only thing on the agenda for the foreseeable future.

At the end of the activity (usually when he was done with it of course) he would rip the Velcro picture off the wall and place it in the Finished Box himself. Eagerly, he would wait at the wall to see what was coming next and repeat the routine. Within a few weeks we could upgrade the visual schedule to two in a row, then three, and so on. This went on to work well for a weekly visual schedule at home because it helped him to arrange the week in his mind – and to this day, still makes a huge difference when he is confused.

*

You know your child best. Working with the professionals to create a team situation only *helps* your Precious. If the professional is not willing to take on board your suggestions (within reason of course) then you may want to consider whether they are appropriate for your child or not. This is advocacy.

Anecdote.

Fortunately, when My Precious was in the process of achieving an official diagnosis (as gruelling as that process is) I was already linked in with a team of early intervention facilitators at a clinic nearby. For my Precious to qualify for the government funded speech therapy (which had a waiting list the size of the Great Wall of China) a new procedure had been introduced where it was mandatory for at least one caregiver or parent to complete a course on speech. Call me lame, but while other parents moaned and groaned, I was secretly super excited! A course that was funded by the local community health organisation, that was going to help me learn about my child's condition... you bet your ass I was excited! (Besides, I was a full-time mum and wife – I looked forward to the adult interaction.)

It wasn't very convenient, however – and it certainly wasn't a simple process. This course was a twelve-week block that involved going to a class between 5pm and 9pm on a weeknight. I would prepare dinner for my husband and our Precious, and the moment Dad walked in the door, I was already running late. In the days following the class, we had to go back to the clinic to show the therapists a live example of what we had learned – using our Precious Ones as our subjects. The sessions were recorded – and replayed in front of the class the next week.

This was challenging. With appointments filling up our days, this was yet another thing I had to drag my son to. It felt almost wrong, to make him perform like a monkey in front of a camera – or for me to have to do the same. Our lives were constantly under the microscope. All for the greater good of course, but at the time – I certainly battled with it. **I was stressed. I was stretching myself so thin.** I was in the middle of some extremely distressing and emotional family stuff at the same time as having to complete this course. By day I was tending to my Precious and his mountain of paperwork that was piling up, his therapies and everyday chores. By night I was sifting through police evidence from the case of my mother's suspicious and sudden death. I was drafting letters to barristers and lawyers and communicating with police officers and the coroner's office, to represent my family and push for a coronial inquest.

But I still went to class. I still went to the appointments to prove what I'd learned. My marriage was straining under the pressure and spawning a lifeforce of issues of its own. I was planning and preparing for the official diagnosis of my Precious, the anticipation building – a live wire dangling until I could somehow connect everything together. I was a hot mess barely managing to keep my head above water... **But I still went to class. I still went to the appointments.**

We all have our shit, life is full of chaos and stresses – a multitude of distractions and abstract horrors and demons we are secretly fighting alone. While we're in it, we just bear down and get on with it. When the dust settles, and the sun comes up again - we can look back and think, "How the hell did I get through that?" *But you did...You do.* **Because you are a Superhero's Superhero. You are the Chosen One, remember?**

No matter how emotional I was driving to that course every week, I would pull myself together in the carpark, walk into that room with other mums (most of whom had their husbands by their side) and all that mattered... was helping my boy. Although I was often distracted, it all fell away when I thought of my little boy who would not get the help he needed if I didn't do this thing. I thought about his little face. How much I wanted so desperately to hear him say, "Mumma". How frustrated and distressed he would become when he couldn't communicate what he wanted to say. The helplessness of not being able to just fix it for him.

This course was called The Hanen More Than Words Program – and it changed my life. **It changed OUR lives.** I don't know where you are in the world, or what resources are available to you – but if you're interested in something like this I recommend getting in touch with your local health services and community centres. (Refer to the back page for a list of courses that I have completed and recommend books and their websites/information.)

To this day, what I learned in that course is still valid to us and still relevant. My Precious didn't even enter the speech therapy program. I was his speech therapist. **Every. Single. Day.** In everything we did, I practiced what I learned. We had fun with it! Before a month was out, he was saying actual *real* words. Before the year was out… he was saying "Mumma". Now… he doesn't shut up! As much as I am a typical mum who has answered 350 questions by 8am and I roll my eyes and tell him to stop talking so much – I must remember back to all that hard work.

I really appreciate that he's annoying the shit out of me with his constant jabber, sometimes I just sit and listen to his words as they roll off his tongue (perhaps with no idea what he's talking about). I really appreciate the fact that my Precious is a regular chatterbox! In five years, My Precious has worked with four occupational therapists at home, as well as two speech pathologists for reviews and reports. He has recently started seeing a child psychologist who specialises in ASD. He has regular reviews with a paediatrician, an ear, nose and throat specialist and a continence clinic.

As he goes to a specialist school, his teachers are well equipped to help him thrive in a sensory-pacifying environment – and I love popping in for a chat or leaving them notes in his diary. Communication here is vital. If I have an issue, I speak out. They are always more than willing to help, support and accommodate. These professionals all know me. I make myself known, and I have huge respect, appreciation and love for everyone that has impacted our lives.

Why do I make myself known? I am in the centre of an ever-growing Rubix Cube of information that makes up my Precious' life. I am what is linking all of these different specialists together who all have one common goal… we are a team working for this one beautiful Soul. Outside of all of this, in my 'spare time' (ha ha ha!) I have read countless theories, research, and stories. I try to stay up to date with the current developments with government funding and community projects.

I have sought out many spiritual interpretations and concepts from some of the most reputable intuitives and gurus, and I also receive my own 'downloads' from Spirit and the Divine Realms. **The best teacher of all –** *My Precious.* And I'm not done yet. I will never be done. I can always learn more. Something I have realised, and that one day you will come to realise about yourself – I am/we are experiencing this for a reason. I am learning, so I can teach, too. I can teach you what I know; the good, the bad, and the ugly. My experience may not be as mainstream or as black and white as you're probably used to, but that's what makes me 'me' – and I hope there is something special that I can give you by sharing my experience with you. In turn you will have your own unique experience, that you may be able to pay forward as well.

My advice to you, dear beautiful, dedicated and loving Soul: **Do the work. Learn, listen, participate, and connect.** Find out whether there are any courses or groups you can join in your local community. Attend the therapy sessions as an active participant and not just an observer. Write it down. Practice it at home. Watch your child. Take photos and selfies every day, these moments go so fast. If you spend just one day trying to see how you Precious experiences their world (which let me tell you, is not the same as your world) I promise you, you will fall in love and admiration of that little Soul all over again… and again and again.

Affirmation

I am willing to let my personal insecurities dissolve

So as I can be present with my child in the moment.

I allow the wisdom and knowledge to come with experience and practice

With total ease and loving grace.

I am the captain of a team who are working together

Toward creating a more empowered and meaningful life for my Precious.

Thank you. Thank you. Thank you.

It is done. It is done. It is done.

Chapter Eight

Making Sense of Sensory Processing

Autism is such a broad subject, and everyone has their own perception of what it means. *Why?* Because everyone is unique, every circumstance is different – and each individual deals with things in their own way. One person with Autism is just one person with Autism – how that affects the individual is different – and how it is experienced by their supporters and carers will be different again.

Although it's certainly a lot more common these days, my personal experiences lead me to believe that some people are genuinely uncomfortable when you mention Autism. This is especially noticeable if someone has been quick to judge your child or your parenting before being awkwardly sobered by the word 'Autism'. I used to get caught up in not wanting to label my child – I didn't want people to judge him or pity him.

That was until I began to endure some of the comments and judgements from others' (ahem) 'unsolicited advice' if you will. Here's some examples I'm sure you've heard – if not, you probably will.

- "Oh, *I* would never let my child do that"
- "You shouldn't *let* him do that."
- "Are you going to *let* your child get away with that?"
- "You're being a bit of a naughty boy – I don't know how your mummy puts up with that behaviour."

Ok Margaret, how would you have me stop him? Should I beat him up? Should I smack the sensory overload out of him? I'm so glad you're the object of parenting perfection, oh wise one! My favourite comment (note the sarcasm) aside from having someone compare my child to 'Rain Man' or 'Sheldon Cooper' is this old chestnut: "He just needs a good smack!" *How about back the fuck off Larry, before I smack you. Right in the eyeball.* (Just some comic relief for you, for getting this far! Of course, I've never said those things out loud – but I have thought about it, and I bet you have too!)

We as parents and caregivers are going through quite enough, it's not cool that we must explain ourselves and justify our parenting strategies… but get used to it – because you'll find you come across it at some stage. People are entitled to their opinion (even if they shouldn't share it, people still do). **It's all about how you handle it.** I make people aware of my child's diagnosis these days, if it's relevant. Not to label him or to minimise him - but to protect him from judgement. I simply say, "He has Autism, and this situation is challenging for him. That's not 'punishment-worthy' to me. I pick my battles".

"So, you know someone with Autism? Great. That is just one person with Autism... no one person on the Autism Spectrum is the same. But thanks for sharing advice about your friend's neighbour's cat's owner's nephew who has Autism. That was helpful..." Most of the time people are completely understanding and strike up a conversation or awkwardly change the subject. Besides, it's becoming so much more common these days, that hopefully you won't have to endure as much of it.

It's not that people don't care or are intentionally being rude – as I mentioned earlier, it's generally the case that everyone's impression or experience of Autism is very different. For the most part the general population has empathy, maybe even a deep appreciation for what you do and what you endure every day. Because, you're amazing. What I find is missing from the general public's awareness of Autism is the Sensory Processing difficulties. It's not the Autism itself that poses the biggest challenges for My Precious, but the ability to regulate sensory information. He perceives it in a unique way and expresses himself in a unique way, and it must be so hard for him to live like that. **I admire him. I love that about him.**

I love that he's 'different'. He amazes me. His resilience, his ability to see things from a such an obscure and deep perspective. I love the way his impeccable memory and outstanding visual perception is completely unique and complicatedly beautiful. I wish I could experience how he feels and sees the world... to better understand him and to help make the challenges easier to cope with. Also, so he would feel less ostracised and lonely with it. I am grateful for my connection to Spirit, and the ability to download information and see things that he has difficulty understanding and expressing. It is with that ability that I am able to share this stuff with you in the first place.

Any therapist will probably tell you, the sensory aspect of your child's everyday life - whether it be to assist in language and speech development, motor skills, behavioural issues, over-stimulation - is a major factor. The best thing I could've done for my Precious in his early years, was to learn more about **how he** sensed things, his 'sensory preferences'. In the meantime, Spirit has insisted I dedicate a chapter of this book to this subject in the lead up to what's next, so...

What is Sensory Processing?

"Sensory processing disorder (SPD) is a neurological condition that exists when sensory signals don't get organised into appropriate responses. People with SPD find it difficult to process sensory information (e.g. sound, touch and movement) from the world around them. This means that they may feel sensory input more or less intensely than other people. SPD can therefore impact on a person's ability to interact in different environments and perform daily activities." – **Kid Sense***

In simplified terms: the way in which the person perceives the world around them and what's going on inside them – is not the same as a 'typically developing' child. Generally, when determining one's Sensory Profile, there are guidelines for where a 'typically developing' child should sit on the scale for their age group. Depending on how the child scores on this test, determines their overall Sensory Preferences. How much it differs from the 'norm' exhibits the severity.

Completing such a profile takes some time. You will need to dig deep and think about what your child typically prefers, to notice anything they do that may seem obscure in terms of their typical age group. Noticing their movements, mannerisms, likes and dislikes, triggers and so forth is a sure way to pick up some clues. My Precious is my first born, so to me everything he did was totally appropriate (aside from the obvious Autism signs). These assessments helped me to see that there were many differences to where he 'should' have been on the scale, and I began to see just how difficult things must be for him. Not to compare for comparison's sake, but to see on paper how challenging he must find everyday things that we take for granted.

In Precious' case, he has always scored toward extremes in 'under sensitivity' – meaning he is under stimulated or under-sensitive to most sensory input and so tends to seek out that sensation. For example, when I was completing the Hanen Program, our homework was to identify our child's sensitivity. I quickly noticed that My Precious didn't seem to feel pain in the same way that I would. He could walk on sharp blocks over and over, as if he felt it was comforting – where I would scream (and swear) in agony.

He would roll on top of things, squash himself under the couch cushions and ask me to sit or lean on him. He would not be able to do everyday tasks without some type of visual cue, whether it be a cue card for instruction and explanation – or the fact that the TV or iPad had to be constantly within view. The list went on, and over time has either stayed the same or become gradually more intense. With maturity and lots of hard work, there are also many things that are still prevalent that he has learned to self-regulate without much intervention…(clever cookie).

As he is a visual Soul – he is often getting 'stuck' on something exciting to the eye. Even to this day he can watch the same scene of a movie or advertisement over, and over, and over until we all want to smash the TV. (He memorises things in this way and learns best through visual stimulation.) He also learns best with visual aids such as images, videos, hand gestures and the written word. I'm sure our family and friends will remember that when they came to our house, there were very clear instructions with (graphic) icons as to how to use the toilet and wash your hands!

Another question I get often, most directly related to his TV and iPad etiquette. "Why do you *let* him do that? That would drive me insane." **Why do I *let* him? Because, he needs to.** Each time he watches the same thing over and over, he is picking up the most intricate details – the mise-en-scène. I don't expect anyone would tell me off for liking my coffee strong and sweet, it's my personal preference. Why should I tell my child not to enjoy his movies the way he prefers to? (Especially if he's laughing and excited and having a grand old time.)

Is it annoying to me? It sure is! But I love that he loves it that way, and that's enough for me. Frankly if people who are visiting don't like it, they learn quickly that unless it's agreed that we watch something uninterrupted together – they need to deal with it. (Respect, remember.) Through these simple things that we can hone in on – we can establish the best way in which our Precious ones learn. We figure out what they need to feel 'regulated', to concentrate and feel calm, or like the movie anecdote – to feel pleasure and enjoyment.

(Try not to get overwhelmed with this part, as you'll no doubt be working with an occupational therapist or speech therapist already who is all over it – and they will be a great resource for you.) If you want to help your Precious in everyday life and you want to start now – I encourage you to do some research, read some books, take some courses. *(See back page for recommendations.)*

Understanding these concepts about how YOUR child experiences THEIR world is **one of the most beneficial things you can learn.** As we touched on earlier, you are most likely the one who knows them best. You are most likely the one who must endure the repercussions of a child who is out of balance or having a sensory overload. It will make your role easier, more rewarding, and make room for so many more pleasant and blissful moments between mother/father/carer and child.

Affirmation

I notice the way in which my child perceives and interprets sensory input

with interest and understanding.

I consciously create new ways in which to help my child to stay regulated

With his/her best interests and preferences in mind.

I see beyond the realms of my own perception to understand,

To love and to empower him/her.

Chapter Nine

Outside the Box Communication – Part One

One of the most common challenges within the Autism world is **communication.** This can take many forms, some obvious and others not so straight forward. Perhaps the most obvious is where a Soul is 'non-verbal' and uses no spoken language. It can also affect one's hearing or auditory receptivity, and the way they can receive communication from others.

The Soul may present with a delay in the production of speech or an impediment with the annunciation and tonality of speech, (and other relevant challenges). When words and sounds are being achieved, there may then be other challenges that arise; such as repeating of sounds and words without appropriate context. For example, my Precious has had a little from all these categories at some stage, and once he was able to produce words he developed what is called Echolalia. (Echolalia is repeating back exactly what they've heard.)

This is cute in toddlers, because they're so little and they're just mimicking what you say. (They may have no idea what they're saying – and they speak with such expression and conviction that it's just gorgeous and you just want to eat them up!) When they are verging on school age and it's still prominent in their interactions, it becomes a little... heartbreaking. I could ask my Precious a question and he would respond with the same question. I could give him a choice of water or milk and he would respond with "water or milk". It took a lot of guessing, reading his expression and body language, and repeating the question and answers very slowly to figure out what he wanted.

It also meant that once I got the correct answer to the question, I then had to spend a little more time reiterating the answer in a full sentence. "You wanted water! Good boy. I want water. I want water." (wait for child to reach for the water) "Water! Yes. Thank you for my water, Mummy." I often still do this, and must sound like I am being condescending, but it has become a natural mechanism – and I do it with my Little Precious as well. (Modelling the behaviour you want them to adopt.) My Precious has also used dialogue from familiar television shows or movies to communicate his needs and feelings in a context that *he* understands, and quite often is relevant to the situation. I have witnessed this with other children on The Spectrum as well, and in those not on The Spectrum. If you think about it, I'm sure you can think of many of your own examples as well. So, let's think about this a little deeper...

Anecdotes.

As previously mentioned, I stayed with a family for a few months when I was in my twenties – who's youngest child was on The Spectrum. His parents had a genius idea to leave Scrabble tiles out for their Precious to play with. One day he seemed to be having quite a hard time explaining what he wanted, and he sat rocking back and forth on the floor next to a few words he had made from his letter tiles.

As I looked down at the image, I could see that he had four tiles turned face down in the shape of a square, with the letters XP beside it. He was becoming increasingly heightened, when I asked him what his picture was. (At the time, Windows XP was the computer software for his home computer – so it took a while to figure out that he was wanting to play on the computer!) "Yes. Windows XP. Windows XP."

Soon after that when I understood what he meant, he grabbed more tiles from his little bag and began to spell more words. "NO TV BEER NO." I was puzzled... Then I remembered a Simpsons episode where Homer says, "No TV, no beer... make Homer go... something, something (crazy)". When I said that quote to him – he again rocked back and forth mumbling it to me – repeating it over and over until finally, the penny dropped. The Simpsons quote and the Windows XP display on the word tiles, along with his elevated and distressed state made me walk over to the family computer and turn it on. The lights were on the tower, but the monitor wasn't on, it was black. The poor cherub couldn't turn the computer on. He couldn't access Windows XP, and it was making him feel 'crazy', just like the episode of the Simpsons where Homer didn't have his TV and beer.

When the computer monitor was turned back on, the issue was fixed – crisis averted. The clever Soul had communicated in the best way he understood how, and with a little deep thinking (and a fond love of The Simpsons) from a nearby grown up, he was finally happy playing on his computer in no time!

*

Excerpt from Unicorn Daydreams (Blog) – 14th October 2017

'Children's innate ability to comprehend...we don't give them nearly enough credit!'

My eldest child continues to amaze me with the profound concepts and knowledge he seems to have about life, despite only being 6. He has many challenges and daily struggles comprehending social cues, needs strict routine and self-stimulates to keep himself emotionally regulated.

But there are so many moments in a day that all of that falls away and he speaks directly from his heart - with concepts and ideas that challenge me, he explains emotion in simple and blunt ways. He has no filter, he can't sugar coat his wisdom, and I love that - even though it's sometimes frustrating, I love it. I try my best to nurture his gifts and to curb them to be a little more socially acceptable, but all in all he is so deep and intuitive that he teaches me new things daily... he raises the frequency in the room with his words.

Recently he lost his dear Poppy, his only stable, consistent grandparent he has in his life. He and his Poppy shared a very unique bond, and when he passed away, my beautiful son shared his words of wisdom that went on to comfort many who were grieving. Since then, he has been almost obsessed with death. Of course, my concepts are probably a bit unorthodox being that I communicate with Spirit, (but I refuse to lie to my child about such things as he has an impeccable memory, and well... he's spiritually aware, so he'll know if I'm not speaking my truth).

After becoming cross with him (unintentionally) about continuing to watch the death scene in The Lion King 101 times a day (and I'm not even kidding...) I tried to explain that sometimes thinking about something sad so often can make you feel sadder. I have given him a good couple of months to process in his own way, but I felt this was getting a little out of hand.

His questions about death are hard to answer because they are so intense. I drew him a picture of Poppy, and of all of us (his family). Each person had a coloured bubble inside them filled with love hearts and photos – 'memories'. I showed him that was our 'spirit,' that is 'our love and our memories'.

Poppy's picture showed his 'love' and his 'spirit' escaping in a cloud from his body - and I said, "Poppy's body has passed away, but his love and his spirit is still here. He can be with us all of the time now. You can't see it, but you know it's there". That has become my new motto for him. "Oh yes, that smell - you can't see it, but you know it's there". I have used it a few times so as he can understand the concept.

Well, the questions were still coming hard and fast, everything and anything could be related to Poppy in some way, and at this stage I'm thinking "Okay, he's stuck on a cycle he can't get out of, he's a CD that's skipping over the same beat. I need to get him off track'. I tried to get him to admit that he needs to begin thinking about happy things and try to leave understanding death for when he's feeling less sad. We talked about angels and other profound stuff - all the while as a parent I was freaking out on the inside thinking, "Far out, is this too much? Can he handle so much? Am I making him more confused?"

Skip a few days and he is consciously saying more positive things, he has been asking questions, but they are related to spirit and love - a whole lot more pleasant than death and dying!

Last night it was 'Movie Night'. He chose to watch The Lion King 2 because it wasn't a 'sad one'. Now, hold on - he has made a conscious effort to change his thought process, he is trying his best to see things in a positive and happy light. THAT is friggin' awesome. Well done son!

So we've got our snacks at hand and pillows and blankies, we're sitting on the couch together and the intro begins. Well, cheese and whiskers, I almost burst into tears! (And I rarely cry these days!) The intro (see link below, and I urge you to watch it) is a visualisation of Spirit, of how Spirit feels to me! And what do you think my boy said to me? "Look mummy, it's Mufasa's Spirit, isn't it? Is that Mufasa's love? You can't see it, but you know it's there?" <insert crying face here!> In my 6 years of parenting, I would put this in the top 3 most touching moments that made my Soul sing and cry at the same time. And that's a hard call to make!

So, what's my point? (Yes, I know - I waffle on - you'll get used to it!)

We often try to protect our children too much. Naturally we want to protect them from pain, shield them from harsh realities and let's face it - make everything rainbows and unicorns even when in life it's not always the case.

If you have little ones (or big ones) or any children in your life, I encourage you to strike up an interaction. Let them talk. Let them think and feel and express how they see things. Let them show you their process. Challenge unhealthy thoughts and behaviours, of course. But watch as they spin you the f@#$ out because they are so deeply in touch with Spirit and nature and all things magical that they will in turn bring you perspective, healing, and an astonishment and pride - that is the most wonderful feeling. Plus, their smiles and laughter are contagious!

Young children are still tapped into their divinity from birth - nurture it, encourage them to hold on to that sparkle. And sit back while they school you with their magic! You can't help but wish you had the perfect, untainted and innocent mind of a child... back when things were simple and new. Maybe you'll learn that it's important to get in touch with that inner child of your own too. Let her/him speak. Love them. Heal their concerns and issues. Play a little, be jovial and silly and let go of adulting for a few minutes... ahhh, what the heck - give yourself a whole day! You'll feel so much better for it.

I share this with love, and hope it reaches the heartstrings of all who it's meant to.

https://www.youtube.com/watch?v=shYouqOEE48

- *Angel Wing*

*

Many children/people on The Spectrum are telepathic.

That is to say: they communicate through thought or other non-verbal methods such as energy exchange or thought transference. Telepathy isn't something widely discussed in our society, but let's 'go there' – shall we? Are you ready? Are you willing to open your mind to the concept? We all have the capability to utilise the gift of telepathy, and very often we do so without being consciously aware we are even doing it. You don't have to be a savant to access this ability, this is innate – it's a natural ability within you right now.

Have you ever thought about someone and then they've called you, or you've bumped into them in the street? Have you ever been down and out when one of your friends has just checked in on you with perfect timing? There has been an energetic signal, sent out and received – a distress signal so to speak. There are times as well, when we have that certain friend or friends who we can just look at and have a non-verbal conversation based on an invisible message that we send through our eyes and thoughts, gestures and expressions. If you're lucky enough, this may be your bestie or your partner – but I'm sure we've all got that one person that we can just connect with and have a telepathic (and generally hilarious) conversation.

Spirit tells me that this is especially prominent in people who are on The Spectrum. More so in very young children and older adults (who have not been the recipients of the assistance that is available now within Early Intervention Programs and tailored Speech Pathology). From their original Soul incarnation, the very first lifetime of the Soul – language and speech wasn't necessary. Souls communicated telepathically and energetically, and there was no need for verbalisation. (We will delve deeper in Soul origins in the next book, for now – let's not go nuts!)

Spirit says: *'As they have entered this lifetime on a similar frequency to where they originated, with the cellular memories attached to that origin – a Soul must then learn this specific lesson... That on this planet and on this dense frequency, they must learn that telepathy is not the primary form of communication here. They chose to be challenged in that way, and oh what a task they have set for themselves! This is an incredibly hard adjustment for these Souls, and it is often met with resistance, fear, frustration and avoidance. It may be incredibly difficult for these Souls to find the right words to express what they are feeling or thinking – or perhaps there are no words in their vocabulary to fit. They may feel like a foreigner in their own skin, with the inability to speak the native tongue.'*

Spirit also suggests that integrity has a lot to do with a Soul's motivation to produce sounds that form words to communicate externally with people. They are not performing monkeys, and they will know what is happening if you try to teach them in a mainstream way.

A non-verbal child will still be able to communicate their needs for an extended period without using any words. They will utilise tones, gestures, eye contact, emotion and telepathy to their care givers. Therefore, care givers and parents can understand what their Precious needs while others may not have the slightest clue the meaning of each grunt or shriek. Some Souls on The Spectrum may never use speech to communicate. This does not mean for a moment that they don't understand the sounds of verbal words – and quite often have so much intelligence and creativity that they are longing to express with you, with the world.

How incredibly frustrating for them! To know exactly what they want to say, and yet their physical body will not allow it. It is no wonder they are having such a hard time. It is no wonder they lash out with aggression, because dammit at least that sensory input helps them to feel something, to relieve some part of them that just needs an outlet for their constant frustration. Every Soul has a way of communicating – whether it be physical, telepathic, or energetic.

Anecdote.

When my son was in the process of being diagnosed with Autism, I would vent to my dad about my concerns and the processes we were going through. From the very beginning of our Autism journey through to the day he left the physical plane - my dear old dad maintained that his first grandchild, his pride and joy, was just 'smarter than the rest of us'.

When I shared my worry that he wasn't producing any words yet, my dad told me a story that soon became his 'go-to' story every time anyone mentioned my son's lack of speech. My old man loved a good old yarn. (I wonder where I get it from?) He'd tell this story, with character, hand gestures, and gusto. (Please excuse some of the inappropriate generalisations, but to be true to the story, it has to go as it does.)

"There was this bloke I know, who knew a guy, who knew a guy...he had a kid and he didn't talk. At all. The kid didn't talk and was about ten... true! Everyone was all stressed out and worried if he was tongue-tied or Autistic or deaf and dumb or whatever. They took him off to the quacks – and the bloke says, he says "nah mate, it's not that he can't talk, there's nothing wrong with him mate.... It's just that he's got nothin' to say. He's got nothin' to say!"

What my wonderfully tactless daddy meant by that story (and believe me I heard him tell it more than a few times) was that the boy in the story was much more advanced, intelligent, profound - than the people around him gave him credit for. Dad's story meant that the boy everyone was worried about was an observer, a witness. The boy in the story didn't feel inclined to justify others with any words. He was so advanced (as my dad would put it) that he had nothing to say on this dense, low frequency. He wouldn't dignify them with a response.

Now, my dad was a very religious man and a very deep and profound philosopher at times – and I always loved it when he told this this story. At first, I didn't know what he meant, but boy did I enjoy hearing him tell it. It was so cryptic and almost like a fable that it always got me thinking (and laughing!)

It wasn't until I began receiving spiritual information and learning about my own child's needs and hidden abilities and intelligence that I truly got the point of his tale, and I suddenly grasped the concept. What he meant was that the boy in the story was on such a high frequency that he had no need for words. He could communicate telepathically, as he had done during his original incarnation. The way in which he perceived the world was so unique, that the world would not need to hear his voice. His energy alone was enough to change the people around him, to change the world.

*

Trigger warning.

This section may be distressing, so please be aware that this may trigger an emotional response about aggression and violent outbursts with our Precious ones. Be gentle moving forward.

Now, whilst it is all well and good for me to say that it's okay that your child doesn't speak or may never speak – that doesn't take away from the reality of it. The truth is, that in this society it is taken for granted that everyone communicates verbally. There's a harsh reality that frustration and emotional outbursts go hand in hand with being unable to communicate one's needs and wants efficiently.

This is something that some parents and caregivers will endure more than others, but it's an important topic that needs to be discussed. Most of society doesn't see this side… This is the shit that happens behind closed doors. This is the shit that snaps a little piece of your heart off every time. This is the stuff that causes us to verge on breaking point – where we just can't take it anymore. It's the pain behind the smile, the lines under the eyes of Earth Angel (who is so bloody exhausted that just being upright is an effort).

This is for the mums and dads and grandparents and carers who cry themselves to sleep. Who hide in their room while their Precious is throwing themselves against their bedroom door and smashing up the house. Who sit on the floor with their arms and legs wrapped around their child as they beat the living fuck out of you, and all you can do is try to restrain them in a sensory-appropriate embrace as you pray for it to be over.

The aggression is real. The pain is real. The fear of self-harm or harming others is real. The struggle, as they say, is real. When our Precious ones have physically aggressive and violent outbursts in fits of frustration and rage, it is gut-wrenching. It is the most emotionally painful physical-hurt one may experience within the realms of the Autism world. What I mean by that, is although you may be hurt physically, there is severe emotional pain caused because you understand *why*, and you may understand *how*, but you are powerless to help it, to stop it. You are powerless to end your child's suffering and beat you up as they may – that is nothing compared to how torn up you are inside over this.

The fact that your child is *so* out of sync with themselves and so overwhelmed with the world, that they have to physically hurt you or your family members – not with the intent to hurt you but because they literally can't help it – this is so much worse than the physical bruises. I have what I call 'battle scars' from being an Autism Mum. I have a permanent black eye, from an occasion where my Precious headbutt me directly between the eyes during an episodic meltdown. I wore glasses at the time, and the piece that rested on my nose indented my eye socket and left a nasty black eye for a month. It has never been the same since.

I supported fat lips and cuts to the face weekly. I often had random bruises show up around my forehead and eye brows from the 'headbutting' days. Back then, my dad used to question whether my husband was violent – and when I would explain that it was in fact my three-year-old son beating me up – I don't think he believed me! I've had chunks of hair ripped out from the scalp. Scratches up and down my arms, bruises to the calves, arms, stomach, back – you name it. I've been winded, punched and kicked in the stomach more times than I can count, and had toys and random items used as projectiles at me almost daily.

The worst injury so far has been a kick to the shoulder from the back seat of the car, that popped my shoulder out and caused lasting damage – to the point where I now must see a chiropractor regularly to avoid it causing severe migraines and neck pain. I don't blame my Precious, and a lot of the time my injuries were caused to me because I put myself on the line so that he wouldn't hurt himself or someone else. A lot of the time I allowed my body to be used as an outlet for his frustration.

My injuries were not caused out of spite or malice – or intent to hurt for the sake of my Precious wanting me to feel pain or punishment. His aggression was a symptom of what he was going through, an action to go with a reaction. My injuries were and continue to be something that pain me because... they were caused from the lack of ability to *communicate.* The inability to understand and perceive such a harsh reality, to be able to *express himself.*

What I have realised over some time, is that the more aggressive tendencies my Precious displays, the more love and attention he needs. At times when I feel like hiding away, or I find myself being a little bit frightened of his reactions or actions – I realise I need to be smart about it. I need to truly listen to him, to 'tap in' to him – to find out what is out of balance and what is making him feel this way. Then, most importantly- DO something about it. Take ACTION.

So, what can be done, how can we find ways for our Precious ones to communicate when they have a hard time doing so?

- Sign language, which is more common in schools and kindergarten nowadays, even on kid's television shows and music (AUSLAN in Australia).
- PECS (Picture Exchange Communication System) visual schedules and cue cards are great to assist in helping to understand your child's needs and desires for the visual learner.
- Social Stories: these are great for helping your Precious prepare for transitions (big and small) new routines, trips and transport, new family members, changes in all areas – the ability to plan ahead and know what to expect (often to *expect* that sometimes plans do change, and that's ok!)

I still use visuals and social stories for my Precious who's almost seven years old. Even though he is great at talking, he still needs assistance with ***expression*** and planning.

All of the things that you have undoubtedly heard of and are currently utilising are great – and no amount of spiritual information on this topic is going to take away from the fact that these therapeutic ideas are absolutely brilliant and helpful to developing your

Precious' speech and communication skills. Team work, remember? Your child's therapists are your new best friends.

Affirmation

I lovingly find ways to assist my child to communicate in his/her own way,

By observing and connecting with them on a Soul level.

With compassion and unconditional love, I understand my child's need to release

And hold them in a healing and calming vibration as they express themselves openly in a safe space.

I have a deep knowing that my child has a unique way of communicating,

And together we discover that with ease and grace.

Chapter Ten

Outside the Box Communication – Part Two

To compliment these therapies, I want to draw attention to other less orthodox methods of communication. This is to assist you in designing your own unique communication techniques with your Precious. It takes visualisation and conscious thought – the intention alone will be a gateway to helping you achieve breakthroughs in the way you can understand each other. Every child is different, as is every parent or caregiver. The aim here is to help you develop the ability to 'tap into' your child's energy, to read it, to translate it, and to communicate back via the same energetic transfer.

You most likely already do some form of this exercise unconsciously but zooming in on it will further develop this skill – and the more you do this, the better at feeling and understanding your Precious one's energy language you will become.

Exercise to use non-verbal communication

Read this through once or twice, and when you get the hang of it, close your eyes and visualise what you have read.

Find that space within, of pure peace and love.

The place where you are not a body, you are a SOUL.

A Divine Spark.

You are a seed of the Creator.

You are pure light and love.

From this space, feel your way to your child.

Sense the Divine Spark inside of your child.

Sense the Soul.

Now you feel and see within your mind's eye, both brilliant, vibrant lights –

Sparks of pure love and peace.

Feel them pulsating and emanating light.

You draw attention to your heart chakra, spinning openly with the warmth of unconditional love.

Sense the heart chakra of you Precious One.

Visualise the way in which it seems to be spinning.

(If you sense it spinning too fast or too slow, use your intention to calm it, to lull it into an even, rhythmic pace.)

You begin to feel the love from each heart chakra well up and pour out.

What colour is this love energy?

As you feel the love between the two of you, rippling from one heart to another, a bubble begins to form and take shape.

That bubble begins to grow, and elongate.

It becomes a vortex of energy that leads from your heart to the heart of your Precious...

The bubble-like tube that extends from your heart to theirs is clear and pure.

This bubble is an energetic connection... a live wire sending signals back and forth between you.

This acts like a portal between you, an exchange of frequency, love, consciousness and thought.

The energy exchanged here in this sacred connection can be felt and translated with ease and grace.

Take a deep breath.

Feel the child's energy begin to permeate through this bubble tube towards you.

What colour is it?

As you see it coming down the tube towards your heart, what does it *feel like*?

Can you feel joy and happiness?

Does it feel grey and anxious?

Are there any words or sounds that are transmitted along with the energy?

(This can be decoded and translated for you and present as 'random' words that enter your mind, or feelings that aren't yours as it enters your space.)

What is your child's energy telling you that he/she can't?

Send your child a message back, even if all that message says…is love.

I SEE YOU. I LOVE YOU. I FEEL YOU.

Acceptance. Support. Understanding. Encouragement. Pride.

Tell them via your energy portal that you SEE them. That you are here for them. The child may surprise you and respond, whether just through your energy connection or with some nice eye contact, or a smile – maybe even a cuddle. I promise you, if you are coming from a place of unconditional love and non-judgement, from a place of integrity – that child WILL let you know they can feel it. Maybe not immediately; but they will, and you will know it when it happens, without a shadow of a doubt.

This energy connection between you and your child or the child you care for – is a sacred space just for you. Spirit advises me that you must maintain a habit of disconnecting this bubble vortex when the interaction is complete. The reason for this is that as a powerful opening, you will be vulnerable to other people's energy, not to mention you can cause each other to feel drained and depleted of your own energy.

To do this, using your beautiful and vivid imagination – simply pull the cord from you as you would unplug a charger from your electronic device. Place a hand over your forehead and the other over your heart and imagine sealing this connection point over with a nice warm layer of loving pink energy (as if it were an invisible patch or band-aid). Repeat this for your

Precious, or if they have participated with you in this exchange knowingly, you may be able to instruct them to do this for themselves. You can connect and disconnect this energy exchange in whatever way you feel is right for you – as this is your personal experience, I have simply given an example for you to draw from.

Eventually, once you have found a routine that works for you and your Precious – you may not want to disconnect from their energy. I find My Precious' energy to be warm and exciting – at times it becomes over stimulated, and I can feel it. I will be able to offer up some sensory related activities to help him to regulate, not just because I can see his excitement – but if I really tap in to his energy, I can feel it. It's necessary for me to 'disconnect' for his own benefit, especially as I work with energy, so you can imagine how colourful my energy can be!

Affirmation

I am consciously and unconsciously able to pick up on my child's energy.

I understand the vibrations of my child's energy.

I visualise the transfer of loving and supporting energy with ease and grace.

Reading my own energy and that of my child comes naturally to me.

We can communicate without words.

I give thanks for this amazing experience.

Chapter Eleven

The View – Part One

Foreword

There's a very likely chance you haven't heard of this before, I certainly hadn't before writing this book! This concept was channelled to you from Spirit and completely infiltrated and intercepted what I was doing at the time. (This is Spirit's way of showing me its importance.) **Before we get into the nitty gritty of this subject, I want to remind you...** You are reading these words because you want to understand, to try to see the 'view' from your Precious One's perspective. Even if it's just theoretical – even if it's 'out there', you're willing to challenge your own beliefs and societal barriers to find answers, insight, connection. You're looking for something that is going to change your lives.

Congratulations for getting this far, that is why you are The Chosen One, and this is no accident.

*

Now that we have begun to scratch the surface of Sensory Processing and Communication (and you've asked your therapists lots of questions or done some independent research) let's delve into what Spirit is calling 'The View'. Hopefully by now, you've grasped the concept that people on The Spectrum have a wonderful (and often misunderstood) view of the world around them and what's going on inside of them. There are lots of resources around to explain Sensory Processing issues, from a scientific, medical, and psychological standpoint – and so too are there many spiritual perspectives I have read over the years.

Most of the more metaphysical explanations I have come across have a similar undertone to the information that I receive from Spirit, and yet there are also many conflicting ideas and explanations. There doesn't seem to be **one** conclusive, rock solid explanation or theory – medical or spiritual. Some may be similar, but I am yet to find two ideas or theories that are *exactly* the same. Why? Shouldn't there just be one root cause and effect to explain it in one foul swoop? It's a bit like religion. So many options and perspectives, but who is *really* right and who is *really* wrong? It's a different experience for everyone, because each Soul is unique. Each Soul experiences and perceives their world through an individualised lens, and one's own private world IS their reality.

My suggestion is that there can't possibly be only one explanation for Autism or for Sensory Processing Disorder - as everyone is Divinely unique. (There are guidelines, sure, but just as everyone has their own unique fingerprint... so too do they have different ways of perception.) In saying that, no one is completely wrong, and no one is completely right. What may be an adequate and proven explanation of Autism and its causes, symptoms, challenges and treatments for one person, will not be the same for the next person.

To imply that the Spiritual information I receive trumps anyone else's, or to even come close to what science and research have established over countless decades of study; would be absurd. **It would be like saying there is only one way to bake a cake.** Every chef has their own technique, they may have allergies and use suitable ingredients based on special diets. There are contributing factors involved such as cooking equipment and temperature differences in appliances. The original recipe could be outdated by now and replaced by some new-age thing that completely blows it out of the water... because the circumstances of the *time* are very different.

Would you bake a cake in a wood oven when you have a gas oven? Would you use an egg whisk when you could use an electric beater? It doesn't mean that the original chef was wrong, or that their cakes were awful – it's just that no one way is the only way

– or could possibly ever be the only way. What works today for one chef, may not work in twenty years for another chef. What the consumers ate then, would not be the same as what's popular or suits the dietary restrictions of today.

In this light, I want you to know that my purpose for this book is not to sway you in any direction as far as which 'recipe' makes up the specifics for *your* situation. It would be irrational for me to promise you all of the answers, and if you seek one person to give them all to you, you're likely to come up empty handed. This is your journey to combining the relevant information, both Spiritual and Scientific, and produce your own tailored assessment and action steps accordingly.

Every Soul is unique.

Individual cases are different. You know your child best. You are in the front lines, you know better than anyone – what works, what doesn't work. You know what's easy, what's hard and what's keeping you up at night. You know deep down what you need to explore. What you *will* get from me, is my honest and heartfelt – vulnerable story – my deep personal experiences. I can share some concepts, practical ideas and my complete support, faith and love for you and your Precious ones. I can be the instrument for Divine information, in the hope that who it is intended for, will find it here.

Resonance.

Your own resonance is particularly important when you are researching and stumbling upon information that begins to take you down a rabbit hole of warped and bizarre ideas (like some of the ones in this book for example). If you are tuned in to yourself and the physical symptoms your body displays when something metaphysical is happening – then you'll know exactly what I mean. If not, and you're a little new to this concept, resonating with something/someone can feel a little like this:

- Skin crawling with goose bumps (the tickly kind, not the scary kind – there's a difference)
- Tingle down your spine
- A deep feeling of truth or inner **knowing**
- Pressure or warmth in your forehead or the top of your head (Third Eye Chakra and Crown Chakra)
- Heart-warming feelings
- The sensation of connection or attraction
- The opening of the heart chakra, or 'heart-warming' feelings
- The sensation of peace washing over you, a state of calm
- Undeniable connection, or even obsession with a topic or theory

- Repetitive synchronicity and manifestation of the same thing, being placed on your path

The list goes on depending on your own unique sensitivities. Basically, your 'Spidey' senses start tingling – and you need to learn to TRUST that, trust it more than what everyone else is doing/feeling. They resonate with their own vibrational match – yours will be yours alone. Therefore, comparisons and 'one size fits all' doesn't apply with Autism, because everyone feels things differently. Autism presents differently in each Soul. The causes and reasoning behind the diagnosis is varied; and so too are the treatments that can assist with the challenges and symptomatic behaviour or related health issues.

Each individual Soul came into this incarnation with an energy frequency that is unique to them. I may resonate with theories and practices for my child that you do not – and that doesn't mean either one of us is wrong – it means that our children and situations are not the same. So dear, sweet Souls – keep reading along, and I hope this resonates with you for your situation (as it did for me when I received it from Spirit). After all, you're reading this for a reason... even if that reason is to rule out what does *not* resonate with you.

What you will learn next, is the energy system of a high frequency Soul who presents with symptoms of

Autism. We are looking at the layers of energy that the high frequency Soul endures every day, that they exist within – the energy fields that they entered into this physical body with. Through this diagram and explanation of each layer (as channelled directly from Spirit) we begin to see how difficult this dimension is for them to be incarnated in, and why they are having such a difficult time adjusting to our density.

We gain insight and deeper understanding as to why our Precious ones may display certain mannerisms, exhibit distressing behaviour and moods, and generally realise that sensory input and energy in their world are often distorting their ability to function – especially when we consider that it is all in conjunction with their unique medical, sensory, and psychological presentation.

Spirit advises me that this layered energy system is not suitable for all Souls on The Spectrum – but can be closely related to those on the 'High Functioning' end of the scale. They have also told me that I will be receiving more information for alternative Views in the future, but this particular system is divinely timed to suit the energy of this period – and will be the most beneficial for Souls incarnated now (2018) and beyond that are between the ages of 3 years and 10 years of age. (Souls born between 2008 -2015 who identify as being on the Autism Spectrum.)

It is through this understanding that you may find an alternative way to help your Precious to adjust to the energy they are in here on Earth at this time, as well as to raise your own frequency with compassion, integrity and intention – and unconditional love.

By understanding this system, Spirit will direct us to being able to read, balance and anchor these energies to ensure your Precious ones are energetically in alignment – and will assist them to fulfil their mission here with more clarity and less frequency disturbance or 'static.'

Take your time, go deep with this, and truly feel your way.

Chapter Twelve

The View – Part Two

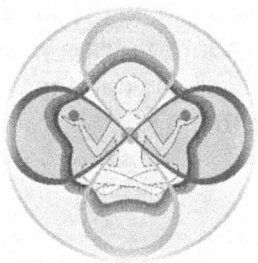

This information channelled from Spirit, relates to a Soul who is incarnated on the timeline between the years 2008 and 2018, who is categorised as being on the Autism Spectrum. At the time of the release of this book, these children will be between the ages of birth and 11 years of age. (As Autism isn't usually diagnosed until the age of 3 or so, I have previously listed it as 2008-2015.)

The reason Spirit has given specific details is because the frequency changes with every moment, and that each Soul being born is bringing forth new energy. The information I have been given is specific to the energy of this ten-year period but will be relevant to these Souls throughout the duration of their incarnation. The children born hereafter may or may not present with the same energetic systems, but Spirit advises that the energy will be considerably different – and so will not necessarily fit the same 'system' or 'energetic makeup'.

There are five 'Energy Layers' as well as four 'Energy Hubs'. The experience of these layers and hubs is unique to the individual – which is yet another reason why it is so important to utilise your resonance and your intuition, as well as your connection to the Soul you are referring to.

Energy Layers

ONE - THE PHYSICAL

The Physical Realm

This is the densest, harshest energy that the Soul experiences.

This is what we can **see physically** around us – the third dimension.

Perceived by the five senses: sound, smell, sight, taste, touch.

This energy is rigid and often hard to endure for the high frequency Soul.

It is hard to endure because the low-density energy does not transmit well, it is hard to compute or translate into a high enough vibration and becomes *distorted* input to the Soul.

It is as if the signal is being sent from old technology into new technology.

Symptoms of imbalance or heightened energy perception/regulation *(may present as challenges)*

- Over-sensitivity to sound
- Over-sensitivity to touch
- Over-sensitivity to visual stimulation
- Over-sensitivity to over-population or crowded spaces
- Preferring to play or be alone
- Over-sensitivity to temperature
- Seeks out extremes with diet (bland, crunchy, or salty and sweet)

- Oral fixations or phobias (particularly with teeth brushing and food textures/temperatures)

Complementary Energies

- Gentle energy healing modalities that *do not* require physical touch
- Meditation and chakra balancing
- Earthly grounding rituals (physical grounding techniques)
- Working with, healing or exposure to the Fae, (Fairies) Mermaid and Dolphin Realms
- Desensitisation/sensory regulation (with guidance from a trained professional)
- Eating a wide variety of grounding foods (e.g. root vegetables)
- Sound healing

TWO - ENERGY IN THE PHYSICAL

Energy in the Physical

Energy within the Physical Realm

This may be perceived as a sixth or psychic sense.

A heightened sense of FEELING is perceived in this energy field.

Relates to the field of energy frequency emitted by *what is within* the physical (energy from people, animals, earth, inanimate objects. The elements – Earth, air, fire, water).

This energy is higher frequency than the third dimension (physical) and is easier to understand and perceive for the sensitive Soul.

It gives clearer input and direct explanation to the soul's innate perceptions. (It speaks in a language the soul can interpret naturally, it's turned up a notch on the dial of high energy, so to speak.)

Symptoms of imbalance or heightened energy perception/regulation *(may present as challenges)*

- Under-sensitivity to sound
- Under-sensitivity to touch
- Under-sensitivity to visual stimulation
- Picking up on other people's feelings and moods
- Awareness of future events before they happen (premonitions and psychic ability)
- Empathy – feeling other people's feelings and displaying the emotions of others
- Lack of spatial awareness, or 'feeling the edges in space'. (Because they are so in touch with

energy it is often the case that they are clumsy or find the human body difficult to get used to)

Complementary Energies

- Energy healing using gentle, subtle energies with or without the use of touch sensation
- Deep pressure on the imbalanced areas of the body
- Working with, healing or exposure to Unicorn and Angelic Realms
- Meditation
- Sound healing/therapy: High frequency sounds (such as dolphins, binaural beats)
- Music and movement
- May benefit from regular, light meals – fresh fruit and salad vegetables.

THREE - TIME

Time

Time

This is a non-linear perspective of time.

Time is seen as an infinity symbol rather than a straight line.

This perception gives the ability to see different time lines at once.

To alter the timeline in the now, ripples change throughout the entire view of time – and so there can be difficulty in 'resetting' the paradigm after an unprecedented change has occurred.

A bird's eye view or 'eagle eye'.

Symptoms of imbalance or heightened energy perception/regulation *(may present as challenges)*

- Struggle to comprehend 'time' in a 3D/linear way
- Distress, anxiety and overwhelm when timelines and plans are disrupted
- The need for a detailed plan with specific detail
- Extremely accurate memory
- Photographic and visual memory and the need for visuals to plan for future events

Complementary Energies

- Working with, healing or exposure to the Dragon Realms and Ascended Masters (St. Germaine, Melchizedek)
- Mindfulness meditation
- Yoga
- Use of 'timer' and daily schedule, visual aids and Social Stories.

FOUR - DIVINE REALMS

Divine Realms

Divine Realms

Another non-linear perspective.

A 'bubble-like' dimension or layer of energy.

Infinite symbol rather than a flat dimension or world.

This realm spins parallel to the 'Time' energy, as if two perfectly balanced infinite symbols are consistently spinning evenly.

When in balance and unison: they spin together at one central point.

This is the realm of Divine interdimensional energies such as Angels, Unicorns, Dragons, Fairies/elementals, Spirit Guides, Extra-terrestrials, Lost Souls and Departed Souls.

This is an extremely high frequency energy, made up of codes that the soul naturally understands and deciphers (like a native language).

The soul is constantly 'tapped into' or 'hooked up' to this realm and can communicate energetically, telepathically and send and receive messages and healing with ease.

This is potentially the most comfortable of the energies for this soul, as he/she remembers what it was like to reside there without physical form.

Symptoms of imbalance or heightened energy perception/regulation *(may present as challenges)*

- May stare off in 'trance' like state for long periods
- Ability to sense the Spirit world (see, hear, feel high frequencies)
- Talks to or plays with 'imaginary' friends
- Fascination or special interest with mystical creatures (fairies, dragons, unicorns etc)
- Communicates with loved ones in the Spirit World (talks as though someone in Spirit is joining the conversation)
- Sees orbs or 'bubbles' of energy
- May present with phobias or fears of 'monsters' or speak about mythical creatures as if they are tangible 'real' beings

Complementary Energies

- Regular energetic clearing and balancing techniques and rituals
- Shielding and connection with Angels and personal Spirit/Animal Guides
- Yoga and Meditation – this Soul is most likely a Yogi and may experience profound visions during dreams and meditations – take note!
- Daily mantras and positive affirmations
- Spiritual guidance, counselling or coaching: lots of support
- Journaling
- Chakra balancing and aura clearing

FIVE - COSMIC / COLLECTIVE CONSCIOUSNESS

■ Cosmic Collective

Cosmic / Collective Consciousness

This relates to the Cosmos, the Universe, the consciousness of all that is.

This is a collective energy that is an integration of all living beings – the overall 'one ness' of all.

The soul can feel, see and download the collective consciousness information and data – as well as to balance, contribute, transmute and send healing to this life force energy.

Symptoms of imbalance or heightened energy perception/regulation *(may present as challenges)*

- Special interest or fascination with space, planets, stars and solar system
- May present with the ability to use technology far beyond the typical capability of their age group
- May present with the ability to take complex electronics apart and put them back together
- Special interests within the topics of science, physics, mathematics, computer coding and robotics
- Innate knowledge of concepts far beyond typical Earthly perceptions and ideas
- Intense mood swings and episodes of unexplained sadness, apathy and depression following a cosmic or global event (even if they are consciously unaware)

Complementary Energies

- Akashic Records and Past Life Readings (possibly regression rituals)
- Healing with divine coding
- Sound Healing (Crystal/Tibetan Singing Bowls, Binaural/Isochronic Tones)
- Numerology and Astrological studies
- Limit exposure to technology and electromagnetic frequency (especially in sleep areas)
- Regular physical exercise to burn off excess energy that stores after downloading constantly (may like balancing, suspending/hanging and being high off the ground)

Energy Hubs

THE VIEW
(The Central Point)

The View (The Central Point)

This is the central point, the crux of everything.

This is the control centre for interpreting the energies in their inner and outer world.

The knowing point – where everything makes sense on a Soul level.

Where everything energetic enters and can be interpreted, sorted out and filtered.

The central point where everything meets: a 'traffic' hub where everything connects and filters traffic in and out.

Perception, understanding and healing through their heart space.

Integrity is felt through this energy centre.

Symptoms of imbalance or heightened energy perception/regulation *(may present as challenges)*

- Frustration and anger outbursts
- Confusion and lack of concentration
- Switching focus from one subject to another rapidly
- Emotional overwhelm or complete sensory shutdown
- Physical aches and pains with no medical explanation
- The need to shut off from affection and interaction (when there may be a jamming of signals at the

centre point and any further input is overwhelming)

Complementary Energies

- Sensory Regulation – tailored sensory diet
- Energy balancing using Unicorn and Dragon energies (Feminine and Masculine – gentle energy for this particular healing)
- Sound-boarding: being able to let the child have open conversations and share experiences that may be obscure or 'other-worldly' (venting/unburdening is important)
- Creative outlet
- Limited processed foods and refined sugar
- Yoga, Meditation, Swimming, Tai Chi, Qigong

THE SPARK

The Spark

Where the soul resides within the physical body. (This spark is inside all living beings.) Zero Point.

The Soul is driving the vessel, it is pure love, joy, bliss and creation.

All lifetimes and lessons, karmic records and knowledge is stored here.

If all energies are in alignment the **Spark** has a communication with the **View.** (There exists an energetic life force between them to transmit and decode all input so as the 'world' makes sense.)

If there is no connection or a skewed connection, Time and Divinity are off balance which stagnates and causes static and poor flow within the View.

Symptoms of imbalance or heightened energy perception/regulation *(may present as challenges)*

- May display severe challenges and delays with speech and comprehension of instructions if the Spark is disconnected from the View
- The ability to 'zone out' into a peaceful state with little effort (if all is in alignment)
- Intense connection to other high frequency Souls with little or no communication
- Places the forehead against things, people or animals that they like

- May display tendencies to hit their forehead or head-bang to relieve numbness, aching or disconnection

Complementary Energies

- Meditation and mindfulness practice
- Bathing in gentle sunlight and swimming in natural water
- Karmic balancing and healing
- Unburdening, venting, creative expression
- Swimming, martial arts, barefoot walking (grounding)
- Puzzles and mathematics
- Systems and computer coding

PHYSICAL FEELING & HEALING

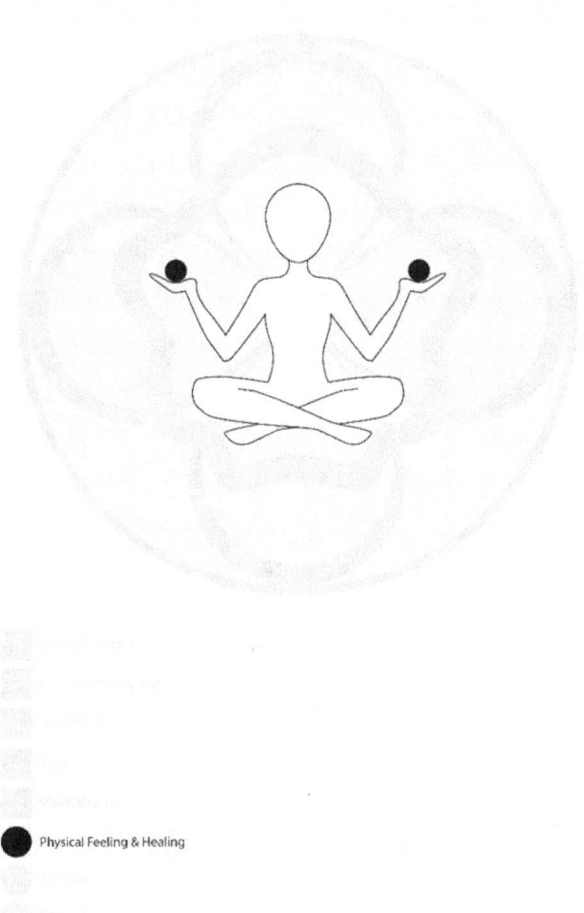

● Physical Feeling & Healing

Physical Feeling and Healing

The sensation of touch is heightened, or under sensitive.

A Soul may feel the energy of all the combining fields with the use of their hands and fingers.

Through the hands and fingers there are receptors to decode and transfer solid/dense (3D) information into higher frequency that can be absorbed, comprehended and expressed, acting as a filtration system.

The expression of emotion flows through the hands and can often result in mannerisms that need constant input or pressure to be expressed or relieved.

The intense energy of this Soul of a healing nature can have profound calming and healing properties when used for this intention.

Symptoms of imbalance or heightened energy perception/regulation *(may present as challenges)*

- 'Flapping' and irregular finger flicking or tapping movements and mannerisms
- Other self-stimulating using the hands and fingers
- The need to touch and feel things in order to understand or learn
- The tendency to squeeze things that they like or dislike, as a way to interpret these feelings
- Having a calming or soothing effect on someone with their touch

- Difficulty refining fine motor skills such as handwriting and using control over their fingers to complete small tasks
- Oversensitive or under sensitive to hands being wet, dirty, sticky, dry etc

Complementary Energies

- Sensory Diet and integration/regulation
- Working with and healing from the Archangels (Archangel Raphael, Archangel Michael and Archangel Christiel) and Fairies
- Yoga, Meditation, Swimming, Tai Chi, Qigong
- Earthly sensory activities (gardening, playing outside)
- Sound healing and balancing
- Companions such as household pets

This information came through as an overwhelming and powerful knowingness – and although it may be different to anything you have seen before – Spirit assures me that this is the best way for us (three-dimensional beings) to understand and visualise the many layers to the energy surrounding our Precious ones. Spirit has given me examples of the way we can see each energy as manifested into the everyday lives of these children/people – and so gives us another perspective as to what may be going on for them.

The examples of complementary energies are merely a guide – as there is an endless ocean of resources for holistic healing, balancing and regulating at your fingertips. Using your child's needs and your intuition/resonance as a guide – you may be able to assist your Precious one to balance the variety of energies that exist within and allow them to restore a clearer, more peaceful state of BEING.

As you may be able to tell, under each of the layers of what Spirit is calling 'The View', we are presented with some tell-tale signs of Autism that we are all familiar with by now. Whilst these qualities are identified as sensory related issues and mannerisms, there is also a very real energetic relationship that ties in very closely. (This is why Sensory Regulation plays such an integral part in the overall balance and wellbeing of our Precious ones.)

Whilst channelling this information, I was almost brought to tears, as though everything finally made sense to me. I personally was able to gain insight into how my Precious experiences the physical and the energetic world all at the same time. (Is it any wonder he has such a hard time? It makes me appreciate so much more, what he achieves every day.) It resonates with me, and I can pin point exactly where my Precious has the most imbalance and what I may be able to do to help him.

For example: My Precious has a limited sense of layer 1. The Physical – and lives more within layers 2, 3 and 4. His high energy means that he finds the physical dimensional energy very difficult to be in – and therefore is under-sensitive to physical sensory input. He seeks out the extra pressure, visual and auditory stimulation – because the average input is not enough for him to feel. There were complementary energies suggested by Spirit through this channelling that I endeavour to try out – because as stated previously – I haven't finished yet. I will always continue to try more to help my Precious.

Chapter Thirteen

What is 'High Frequency' – really?

One night I was sitting on my bed, contemplating how to spend my few hours of 'free time'. The children were in bed for the night, I'd had my hot shower, and I was tempted to call it a night from sheer exhaustion. Usually this was my time for 'work'– the non-mum-stuff like study, writing, and communicating with Spirit. I was in a bit of a slump, and I had been avoiding writing this book for a few weeks…

The energy in my home had been static, emotions were high, and my Precious had been displaying some extreme behaviour. I'll be honest, I was struggling (because I'm real, remember). I kept wondering, "How can I help people with this stuff when I can't even get it right myself?" In the strive for perfection, I had forgotten that it is through my experiences, pleasant and unpleasant – that I am in a real position to be able to help people. Yet, as I was battling some egocentric, lower feelings and thoughts I refused to do any writing – as I was adamant to keep this book as pure, positive and high vibe as possible.

This night, after a rough few weeks of tantrums, screaming fits of rage, door slamming and tears, my Precious had just turned a corner. Something amazing had happened – there had been an energetic shift (finally) and I was just revelling in that feeling of amazement, gratitude – and celebration of the 'win'. Suddenly while I was in this state of gratitude and deep contemplation, Spirit decided it was a good time for a 'download', for me to receive a message. In perfect alignment with my trail of thought, Spirit insisted that I jot it down, and that what I was receiving was specifically for this book. (Nice way to kick my butt back into gear there, Spirit. Love your work!)

I willingly typed it all into the notepad on my phone, and before I knew it, I'd been sitting there for over twenty minutes with oodles of writing on the screen (and a slight case of RSI)! The information was clear and synchronistic – the answer to a few questions I had been pondering about my parenting, and about my Precious. When things are tough, or when I find myself in 'cranky mummy' territory and face that old chestnut – 'mummy guilt', I often talk to Spirit. I ask questions, I unburden myself of all of my shortcomings and I guess you could say, I pray for help.

Spirit never disappoints, even if it is to give me a swift kick up the arse and tell me to stop feeling sorry for myself. (One time during a verbal tug-of-war with my Precious I got a little carried away with the momentum of it all, when I was interrupted by Siri, the voice command on the iPhone. Siri said, "Now, there's no need for that". I freaked out so much - that I'll tell you what: I barely said a word for the rest of the day!)

Most of the time, Spirit has timely advice that is completely obscure to anything I could come up with on my own – and when it's as powerful as this I am also encouraged to share what I have received. Holding myself to that part of my Mission, below you will find a 'transcript' of what I received that night. This is the unfiltered channelling from the Divine that I wrote in my phone (you will see why the joke I made about RSI was not really a joke after all).

"The Soul-contracts of people on The Spectrum often relate to raising frequency; opening up closed hearts to unconditional love. They may possess profound abilities, to ensure they can achieve their Mission. They often 'come in' with highly sensitive energies of a high frequency, and as such, they can quite easily be 'dumbed down' and lowered as they quickly absorb the lower energies around them. These lower energies block their potential and cause 'undesired behaviours' to emerge and or escalate if not kept in tune and cleared.

Often Soul contracts of these individuals are the embodiment of many lifetimes of lessons in which they have become well educated (or even Masters) in a particular field of specialty. They bring this knowledge forward with them into this life for a very specific purpose, this is why they are here on this timeline.

Some of these attributes and gifts relate to (and often not limited to one)

- Mediumship and the ability to communicate with Spirit and other Higher Dimensional beings
- Profound Healing using energy, frequency and touch – often appear to have mesmerising eyes when eye contact is established.
- Healing others; by absorbing lower energies from people and places and transmuting it into a loving and peaceful one.
- Inter-Dimensional, Spatial and Psychic perception – the ability to see the outcome well in advance – and often alter that reality.
- Telekinesis
- Telepathy
- Empathy
- Intense and Immense focus toward the outcome they see, feel and desire
- Connection to plants and animals – the ability to communicate with living things such as trees and birds, dolphins and pets.

- Healing through the elements.

It is integral that someone who embodies such abilities, gifts and energies has regular balancing and clearing in order to maintain stable and continuous flow and emotional regulation. These can be achieved in a number of ways, depending on the individual and the situation or circumstance.

We will teach you how to tap into these needs and how to best clear and assist your child to learn to do so for themselves. This practice, if learned from an early age – can act as a self-awareness and self-help system for your Precious Ones to be empowered: to gain control over their energy and physical body and allow them responsibility and independence for themselves."

Confused, much? If this is hard to understand, I'll try to elaborate for you. What Spirit was saying is that despite physical and psychological 'set-backs' or Earthly 'delays' – these High Vibe people are extremely sensitive and powerful energetic beings. They are often magnetic, drawing in energy and drawing people's attention or stirring feelings within others just by being in their presence.

The more out of balance they are (energetically speaking) the more challenging it can be for them to function in the physical realm. Due to their high frequency and tendency to absorb lower energies, they may have attachments and stagnant energy that lingers in their auric field that impacts their behaviour and moods.

No doubt you'll be familiar with energy healing work such as Reiki, Pellowah, Healing Touch, Therapeutic Touch etc. – this is the healing, removal and clearing of energy. Energy workers are on the rise, because the global consciousness is calling for it – the need to cleanse, balance and heighten our natural state of clarity and purity. It is becoming well known that the human body has the ability to heal itself. Get ready for a whole new wave of different modalities that are about to enter our reality, because it's happening.

There are many types of chakra clearing techniques and meditations you can find either online or in music and book stores, and these are just some of the ways that one may choose to try and assist themselves (or perhaps their Precious) to balance their energy. I cannot recommend any specific energy work for your situation – but I do encourage you to do some digging, find what resonates with you and your Precious. It's also trial and error. What works for one period may not work the next, as energy is a continuous flow, so it's best to keep an open mind!

I remember buying my Precious a few meditation CDs when he was a toddler. At first, they were to help him sleep, and as it was such a difficulty for him at that age – I'd originally purchased them to help him relax (as I was trying to induce some melatonin to occur naturally). I found that he preferred the high-pitched sounds of dolphins (which to me were ear piercing!)

Eventually these became so successful that I packed them in his bag at day-care and kinder as a tool to assist with regulation if he needed some time out or was over stimulated. The educators ended up getting some of the same ones for routine meditation time in the centre for all of the children, and you'll find that these days it's part of a lot of school curriculums. You're never too young or too old for meditation, and simply the act of tuning into yourself is healing and soothing for the Soul.

I have discovered with the help of some mentors, Spirit and my personal Spirit Guides, that working within the realms of Divine energy frequency helps my child to clear and balance his energy *considerably*. So much so that this book is just a prelude to the next – which will be primarily focusing on healing and balancing through energy. Stay tuned! (Do ya' get it? Stay *tuned*? Ha! I crack myself up.)

Still struggling with the concepts of frequency? A few days after the first influx of information came through for this book, Spirit barraged me one weekend with an alternate explanation of what they mean by 'frequency'.

"Think of your latest television set... It has high definition, all of the high-quality sound and spectacular capabilities to transmit signals from the internet (which one cannot see, hear, or touch) and displays viewing in a clear and sensory manner.

Now think of an old transistor radio. It has numerous channels of which a dial is used to manually change frequencies to pick up a signal that plays music and audio that you can easily listen to – yet it is limited in its technology in this modern age. You must consciously dial in to the frequency you desire.

Imagine if you tried to play your television shows through your transistor radio. Would it work? If you somehow created an input into your radio and connected your television to watch a video streaming from the internet, would it translate into a sensory-usable language for you to enjoy? No. It would likely combust. Sparks may fly and there would be nothing but static, if anything at all.

Imagine your Precious One is the television set, the average human incarnation in three-dimensional linear time is the transistor radio, and the internet is The Divine, the connection to Source. If you're like many here on Earth at this time in your Spiritual evolution, you may have Internet-Radio... you are a human being who is linked in with the Divine: within the limitations of your 3D bodies. They have 'tuned in' to a higher frequency by choice or subconscious intention.

The television speaks a language not yet developed for the radio – and the radio thinks that the television is 'different' or 'strange'.

Can you try to alter the television's technology to become more like the radio? It would be near impossible. That would require a system that pulled itself apart to move backwards in its own evolution. Is it possible that the radio can be altered to be more like the television, to upgrade its software and undo old programming to somehow meet the frequency of the high-tech television? That's more likely now, isn't it?

When the television is tuned in perfectly – you get a perfect picture and sound. When there is interference – something has messed with the energy transferred in and out, the signal is compromised. The connection to the internet may become skewed.

In order to maintain a high-quality picture, we must keep the connections clear of interference and distortion, for the television to do its job as it's designed to. So, too – are your Precious Ones in desperate need, not only to be kept in tune with themselves and Source, but they are in need for the world of 'transistor radios' to switch their dials up a *few notches in order to understand and translate their frequencies.*

All children innately possess higher frequency than the generations before. As more incarnate on their Mission within the physical, the need for the generations before to 'wake up' or 'tune in' is necessary. Change is already here, just look to the children."

*

During the process of editing this book, I was decluttering my desk space when I came across a hand-written piece of paper with a channelling that I had received back in 2015 (before I even realised I could channel). I had been looking for this piece of paper – intentionally – for at least a year. No surprise that I came across it, still attached to a notebook that I had already scanned through page by page a few times… staring me in the face. It is so relevant that I was inclined to skip back and add it in here. (Divine Timing…it's a thing.)

It was written when my Precious had recently received his diagnosis, and I was only vaguely touching on my mediumship capabilities at the time. I was frantically cleaning the house and I was reeling over a conversation about labels that I had been having over Facebook earlier (note to self, don't ever put your opinion on Facebook unless you're prepared for everyone to chime in and make your opinion meaningless and trivial).

I questioned what I assumed were my guardian angels at the time, and my spirit guides – and I asked the question… "Why are there labels? Why is any one child more 'gifted' or 'special' than the other?" The thought that perhaps this term 'special' was just a ditch attempt at making us Autism parents feel better, and I was confused what that meant for other 'typically developing children'. Suddenly I heard a clear voice in my head tell me to stop what I was doing immediately and "write this down". I really wanted to keep cleaning while Precious was at daycare, but the voice was pushy. "Write this down, now." Here's what I wrote down…

"Each one born, paves the way for the new. Each one is special and plays a part in raising the energy. This new energy has been successfully raised so much that the frequency of the new children now is more paralleled with the new energy set forth by the previous.

They will raise the frequency again for the next new Souls who will parallel that frequency and so on. Evermore, the future's frequency begins to grow so as to be one with the Divine (the Divine that dwells inside all who live on the Earth).

So it is; each one is gifted, is special in their own light – making waves (so to speak) to bring in new beings with more light and more love than the previous generation. Some bring the light, some hold the light, and others hide from it. Each Soul has the potential to bring peace, love, and unity to all... and in so doing, each one is 'Divine', and 'Special'. Each one are Gifted Creators – and serve their purpose towards the Greater Good. The increase in frequency attracts future high frequency beings, and so forth.

Does that help to answer your question, Dear One?"

I had written my own response beneath – "Many thanks – it was unexpected but thank you for your prompt response. I love you and thank you!" The page after was a rough sketch that I had drawn as the channelling was followed by a vision I received of My Precious. He was riding a giant butterfly and looked to be the age of a teenager or young adult. He was wearing armour with a butterfly symbol on the chest – and it was dated 31/05/2015.

Reading this now, especially after looking for it for a long time, I can see that the principles that Spirit has always told me (relating to frequency and Autism) have always been the same. I hope that you are beginning to get a handle on what this all means, and can put into context how energy, frequency and vibration are all so important... not only for understanding and working with Your Precious – but yourself as well.

Affirmation

I consciously "dial in" to a higher vibration, a higher frequency now, with ease and grace.

I am consciously aware that my children are sensitive to energy, as am I.

I am capable and willing to assist my child to clear and regulate their energy, specific to their needs.

I am a conduit for grounding energy, love and peace, for my child, for myself and for the Highest Good for all.

It is done.

It is done.

It is done.

Chapter Fourteen

Grounding

You may have heard this common term before, especially if you're familiar with meditation and spiritual practices. It has certainly been discussed within different circles of people I have been involved with, and the term gets thrown around loosely online within spiritual groups and pages on social media. I always wonder what it means to people individually, because really – I only know what it means to me. I've learned different grounding techniques at workshops and from various mentors in different meditation circles, as well as what I have read when I have researched the topic for myself. Like many other spiritual practices and techniques, there is a world of information at your fingertips; most of the time you can find what you're looking for online or in books.

Different people and spiritual leaders will have differing opinions, rituals, techniques and so forth. I have found that what works for one Soul may not work as well for another, and it is only *you* who knows what grounding means *for you*. Just as what I believe and the visualisations I have when I am practicing this ritual or method, may only work for me. To me; the essence of grounding is about **connection and unity**. Through visualisation, intent or action, it is the reconnection between yourself and Gaia (Mother Earth) as well as the Great Central Sun (I also refer to as Source). It is the act or visualisation of recreating the fluid, pure, light and loving bond of energy between you and the Universe – until you are connected consciously and unconsciously.

Grounding unifies you with our beautiful planet (or rather, *re*unites you) as we are indeed all one in the same - we are all connected to the Earth, to Source and to each other. What happens to Gaia happens to us. What we are going through, so too is Gaia. What you are going through, so too is the rest of humanity. We are so deep in our forgetfulness that we have become separated from Source, from our Gaia, from each other, and from ourselves. Can you feel that?

We tend to see ourselves as separate entities – even within ourselves we have disconnection between our polarities, our physical and our spiritual. It is no wonder the world appears to be in chaos! Can you see the reflection of that as you look around? People scurrying about – consumed by themselves, their addictions and their desires. The ego is driving them to chase the things that matter the most; which are the same things that only aim to buy them a state of peace and happiness anyway. Can't we just skip to the 'state' of being and BE peaceful and happy now? When we're disconnected from ourselves, Gaia, and Source... that may seem impossible. We're just running around like ants in an anthill.

Then, think about Natural Disasters – when we purge, clear and cleanse all that no longer serves us, both on an individual Soul level and a collective – so too does Gaia. This is also how healing, balancing and being in tune with oneself has a profound impact on the Collective and the planet. Grounding is important, because it brings you back 'to Earth' or rather – unites you so that you can operate in sync with the energies around and within you. I tend to need grounding after major life changes, during extremely elevating circumstances or severely depressing situations. Whenever anxiety or panic begins to surface – I find it balancing and energising to employ some grounding techniques. It also reduces the severity of the symptoms of change, as there is a more natural flow of energy.

As mentioned previously, everyone will have their own version of what grounding means, and this is just my personal view and what it means for me. Have a think about it for yourself as you explore these possibilities – because as you move forward on this journey – you're going to come back to this, probably a lot.

Grounding

The remembrance of our sovereign connection –

The awareness that there is no space where you end, and Gaia begins.

A remembrance of our innate connection.

The dissolving of the *illusion* of separation.

I was once told that if you complete a proper grounding practice – and you do it wholeheartedly and appropriately – that you should only need to do it once in your whole life. That was contrary to anything I had ever read or been taught at the time; and the concept shocked me a little. I was relatively new to the awakening of my spiritual side, and I'll admit I believed almost everything I heard. It's not that I don't believe that advice now, I think there is some truth to it, but I also think that it doesn't quite compute with my own personal journey.

I participated in a group 'grounding' meditation with my Mediumship Circle and it was extremely powerful. To be honest, it was the most powerful grounding I have ever experienced – and it truly lasted about two years. That is to say; I felt as though my feet were firmly planted on the ground, and I was in union with the Universe without the need to keep practicing a grounding technique… for two whole years. But then, my life took a turn and I went through some major upheavals. **I realised later, that once in a lifetime grounding - didn't fit right… not for me.**

Energy is ever-changing and adapting. It is lucid and flowing – and it can be a powerful force, with waves so intense at times that it seems to aim directly at you – as if to deliberately knock you off course. Every trial and tribulation carries vibration and energy, as do the positive and blissful events in our lives. If the roots are planted deeply, then you surely stand a good chance of staying grounded through these violent energy storms.

My Energy

I work with energy; I am a conduit for it, I give and channel energy. I absorb and transmute it. I am an empath – I *feel* everything. I allow my energetic field to merge with the Divine so as I can be a channel of love and light for my fellow human, planet and collective consciousness. I've always been an 'overly-emotional' person, and I have faced some darkness within my own psyche that has been extremely challenging, but also very enlightening. Part of being emotional and, let's face it – a little 'cray-cray' early on; has forced me to be extremely analytical of myself. I am self-aware, and I hold myself accountable for my feelings. When working with energy, it is important to know which 'stuff' is mine –

and which is not. I feel everything so deeply that when it comes to my own stuff, I can appear to be a little switched-off. When I love; I love fiercely, whole-heartedly and passionately (which can often overwhelm me to a state of cold – needing to temporarily detach from the intensity of the feelings as they can too much to bare). When I feel grief or hurt, it is excruciatingly painful, to a degree where I am numb – appearing to be tough skinned (when in fact I am just in shock from the sheer intensity). Because I am analytical and clairsentient – I can generally solve my daily woes and detective the shit out of what's going on within my energy field, and by now, I've got it down!

My journey so far has taken me travelling through some turbulent storms, of which I am proud to say I managed to weather and come out the other side. But I'd be lying if I said that during the process I didn't become a little unhinged, that my pain didn't cause some uprooting of my solid connection with Source, Gaia and my 'higher' self. With that in mind – I could lead you on a guided grounding meditation that you only have to do once in your life… But how can I ever say to you, dear one – that you will *never* become unstuck? How can I tell you that my way is the only way – when you are a unique and vibrant Soul with your own emotional, psychological and sensory preferences? You have your own unique energetic blueprint. My way works for me, but yours may be different.

So, whilst I wanted to stay away from this topic in this book (as it is much simpler to discuss such matters in person while connected with the individual's energy) – Spirit insisted I dedicate a chapter to grounding, and here we are. Spirit implies that it is not only to assist you in being solid in your own foundations, but to help you be firmly stable for your Precious. If you are in unison, completely solid and balanced, you will be more capable of being able to balance and anchor your Precious One's high energy. (And to handle the intensity of it all.)

I will draw the line at telling you *how* to do your grounding practice, because as stated earlier – I believe this is a very personal and individual process that needs to be discovered by you. All you need to know is *what* you're trying to achieve (unity and connection to all that is, and to be in the flow with the Universe) and a few examples of visualisation techniques. It will then be up to you to do your own Soul-searching. Dig deep and think on what grounding means to you – and how best you will be able to achieve this for your own personal journey. Do some research and seek out others who may have something to offer you along the way.

Here are some examples you may like to draw from when you are discovering your visualisations:

The Golden Light of Source

Imagine a golden light pouring down into your Crown Chakra.

It flows to you from Source – bringing with it light codes of pure bliss and love.

As you feel it travel down through all of your chakras, it cleanses and nourishes them as they spin with activity.

As the golden light of Source travels through your light body, it fills you with Divine joy and peace.

As the light travels down through your energy portals, you witness it, as it passes through to the Earth Star Chakra under your feet.

It continues down through to the Earth's Core and you begin to feel your feet being pulled downward with it – as it anchors you to the ground.

The light comes back around in a full circle as it travels through the Central Sun and back down to your Crown.

Visualise this process until you can feel the connection within your physical body, the sensations of peace, love and a clear connection.

Feel your feet heavy on the floor/ground beneath you as though you are magnetised to the Earth.

Tree Root Visualisation

Sit comfortably with your feet firmly on the floor/ground.

Imagine the soles of your feet sprout roots and begin to burrow their way into the Earth beneath.

As these roots travel below, so too are there roots travelling upward from the Earth toward your feet.

Allow your tree roots to intertwine with those of the Earth, enwrapping themselves into a beautiful harmonious entanglement.

As the Earth's roots travel up and up, you feel them begin to enter the room and wrap around your feet.

As the roots reach your ankles you feel the pull as you are tightly planted to the ground.

Physical Grounding Rituals

- Place your bare feet in the soil, sand, water or grass anywhere outdoors. Visualise a connection ritual that resonates with you (let your mind wander – this is the visualisation of your highest intent!)

- Swimming in the ocean and being one with the natural elements – extra powerful with the intention of grounding.
- Gardening and placing your hands and feet in the soil, also especially powerful with the intent to ground yourself.
- Sit beneath a tree (have conversations with plants and animals telepathically)
- Consuming root vegetables or vegetarian diet.

These are merely a few examples – and I would encourage you to seek out what works for you. There are countless guided meditations available online, in audio format and in class workshops and meditation circles, if you need any specific assistance.

Affirmation

I am one with the Creator

I am one with Mother Earth, Gaia.

I am one with the Collective Consciousness.

I AM connected.

I, the Soul – am in the flow with the Universe.

I am Grounded. I am Anchored.

And so it is.

Chapter Fifteen

Anchoring

You may have heard the common term before, **Anchoring.**

Just when I thought this book was almost complete, I kept hearing and seeing the same theme repeat itself in my physical life. I found myself saying this 'random' word that was not previously something that was part of my vocabulary. This is common with my relationship with Spirit, I often get distracted by the physical world and occasionally I miss the signs and messages I am given. They are forced to get creative, so I can receive what it is they are sending. (See, I am real!) When this type of obvious repetition happens, and I eventually catch on to the synchronicity – I recognise this repetition is the trademark of the mysterious workings of Spirit. (Not so mysterious *now*, Spirit – I'm onto you!)

I talk to people, and I talk – a lot. (Sorry 'bout it.)
I found myself saying things like: "He's an *Anchor.*

She's Anchoring him. He needs grounding. You're my anchor. I'm holding the energy like an anchor." It seems obvious now, of course – but at the time I was probably thinking I was just really clever, or that I was just suddenly getting in touch with my inner sailor. I was in fact being guided and influenced by Spirit, and this is what happened (when I finally realised…)

*

My Precious had entered a sudden phase, and with it came a major attitude shift. (At the time of writing this book, he is currently still going through this 'phase' and it's… testing, to put it lightly. Trial and error, forward march!) At first – it seemed to be a 'hormonal' change, and it could well be. He's developed new mannerisms, and new language. He has begun to treat me like his personal gofer and shouts and cries hysterically when he doesn't get his own way. He's becoming increasingly aggressive, and I am currently tailoring some healing that is specific to his current energy needs. (The usual energy work I do for him isn't working right now, so it's a constant work in progress.)

He's particularly sensitive to the energy he receives from digital input (TV, images and movies from what he constantly engages in) and the people he interacts with. He always has been a highly sensitive soul. As I focus on my own sensitivities, I realise that I have been receiving frequency upgrades and overwhelming downloads recently, due to the current energy influx into the planet. The dial is turned *way* up right now, and for my highly sensitive Precious – he would be feeling it too.

Let's get one thing straight; I'm no stranger to the emotional upheavals of my Precious. I can tell the difference between 'Autism' or sensory related behaviour, energy imbalance or interference – but some of these outbursts are just your average attitude problem. Some of these behaviours are just typical six-year-old tanties. It's fun. (Note the sarcasm.)

Of course, I check myself first; what is going on with me – how am I feeling? Is he picking up on *my* energy? I do my Mini Mum-Meditation and find my zero point. I can be calm as a summer breeze and yet he is still flying off the handle over the smallest thing and losing his shit when I have anything to say at all. I can do no right, say no right, and heck – I can't even breath without it being an argument. It almost seems as though he is having episodes of oppositional defiance. (Enter stage left, psychologist to the mix of therapies… because this one is getting serious!)

It's a hard balance between Autism-Mum (understanding and excusing challenging behaviour), Spiritual-Mum (who knows energy plays a part in the human condition) and being a push over for a kid that knows exactly how to abuse the system. (He's on The Spectrum: he's not stupid.) He knows exactly what he's doing for the most part, and holy moly he's darn good at what he does. He schools me constantly. Reverse Psychology? He is a professional at using my own techniques back at me, and half of the time it takes me a while to even notice what has happened. I have met my match for sure! It comes with a bitter-sweet pride, because it shows that he is super intelligent, and his comprehension is outstanding, but man is it frustrating!

I've tried emotional regulation techniques using coloured pictures and coloured zones – (The Zones of Regulation, see back page for references). I continuously encourage a Sensory Diet. I've increased the emphasis on Respect Tickets and the Bonus Prize as motivation. I've tried cutting out certain foods and introducing more fruit and less sugar, salt, lactose blah blah blah. (Note: none of these seem to work for long because he's big, and smart – and he can reach the top shelves in the cupboard and the supermarket. When I get a handle on it at home, he's good at negotiating at his dad's house, school, visiting and parties etc. (Good food choices are something even adults struggle with – so this one may take some time!)

I've connected with his energy and his Spark, and now it seems to be 'working' less than usual. Last week he was having an emotional outburst because of a slight change in plans, and I asked calmly,

"Where's your Spark? Can you feel my Spark?" Precious glared at me angrily and pretended to grab my Spark and smash it up, using his talent for mime-acting. "I'll destroy your *damn* spark because I've had enough! Enough of you trying to make me feel better!" Although I was seething at the tone of his voice and the attitude – I was mostly trying not to laugh. He inadvertently admitted that if he had have gone along with that little routine it would have made him feel better, and the acting was brilliant! Gold star, kiddo… you're not fooling your Mumma.

I said, "Oh, ok…well my Spark is indestructible mate, and I hate to tell you this but… so is yours. Are you just feeling like you like being angry? Do you want to just be angry and mean all the time? Because, it's a choice – you're making a choice to talk to your mum this way. Do you think you are making a good choice? Do you think it's respectful? It doesn't make me feel very good. It's okay to be angry, but it's not okay to let your anger hurt someone".

After some more foul attitude and continued challenging behaviour, my patience was wearing really, *really* thin. (You know those days where you've tried everything, and your bag of tricks is empty, and this has been going on and on for weeks now… you throw your arms up in the air and think 'what the actual fuck, man?' I know **you know** what I mean, I know you just giggled. That's where I was at. That's where I am at a lot lately. You get it, you've been there – just got to ride it out! Trial and error.)

I asked him whether he had been watching YouTube videos that he knows he's not allowed to, threatened to take away all of his technology and any and all of the last resort things we say when we're in that state. As the conversation became an argument, Precious dropped a swear word. (You're probably not surprised where he got that from... BUT in my defence, it wasn't a word that I say often.)

It's always an eye opener when your child swears. It is for me, anyway – because he doesn't usually do it. He's not *allowed to* because he's not a grown up yet. Because even though mum does it – ahem... a lot - it's against the rules for him. He's a good boy, and he's a stickler for the rules. This is not like my Precious.

When I enlightened him calmly that he had just said a 'swear word', he burst into tears and said he was sorry, and that he didn't know. (Bless his little cotton socks, even though he knew it was cheeky and used it in such a way deliberately, he genuinely had remorse for swearing because deep down – he doesn't want to break the rules.)

I sat down with him and told him it was okay, and that I understood that he didn't realise he had said a swear word. I then had to explain what the swear word meant and that it wasn't a nice thing to say. I also apologised because I swear, a little too much. I gave him the old "I know Mummy says some swears

– and I'm working on that, but I'm a grown up…" then he abruptly intercepted. "I know you do, but it's not you Mummy, a boy from my school said it, so I thought it was okay cos he's not grow'ed up."

(Oh my, that was unexpected. Not me after all for a change. Winning.)

I wanted to lecture him on who he shouldn't be hanging out with, and then I realised that it was entirely up to him to make that call. All I could do was shine a light on whether <u>he</u> thinks these friends are making good choices or not. If he likes to make good choices and they don't – then it might be a ***good choice*** not to repeat what they say and do, or to find new friends who make better choices. (Gah, I can't believe we're at this stage already, man! Wasn't it only five minutes ago that I gave birth to him?)

It reminded me of conversations – well, lectures, I had with my parents when I was younger. "That girl is a bad influence on you, you're not allowed to hang out with her anymore. If I find out you are, you're grounded." (Funny, now looking back. Grounded…Touché Spirit, you walked me right into that one.) So, we went back over what had been transpiring for him in the last few weeks, discussed the rules and consequences for those types of choices and then we hugged it out. We spent some time talking about each other's feelings and about good choices.

Did it fix everything? Not really. Like everything it's a process. It's a work in progress, but it was a good start. It did get me thinking about how easily led he may be, and that's a worry for all parents. It's especially perplexing when your child is highly impressionable and perhaps just enjoys any and all interactions from his peers. He is at the age where he is no longer dependent on mummy to choose his friends for him, and so I imagine this doesn't come very easily to him.

Wherever we go and whoever comes to visit - I pay close attention to how Precious behaves around other people, and how his mood and attitude changes whilst in the company of others and how he behaves once they leave. At this point I was looking for evidence... energy evidence.

Recently, we were visiting one of my best friends when I came to realise what the Spirit was saying. Precious was playing Minecraft on the Xbox with my friend's youngest daughter, who is only eleven months older than him. They were in their own little world, laughing and carrying on at the screen and having a ball. I loved seeing him so comfortable, so quirky and comedic – the laughter and the interactive banter between them. It's not something I've witnessed much for him, as a lot of his peers find him a little difficult to play with or his conversations are hard to follow.

I realised that 'Mindy' is his very best friend, probably his only real friend outside of school. Mindy is the only child in his life who he has that rapport with, where he can really be himself. When Mindy and her sister spend the weekend at our house every so often, he never wanders far from her, or needs time out or to hide away in his room.

Mindy has always had 'a way' with Precious, even when I haven't. She could tell him to do something in a quiet little monotone voice and he would just do it. If anyone but Mindy took his toy, or his iPad or changed the TV channel – there would surely be a meltdown or some type of standoff. But with her, he would gracefully give up the shirt on his back without question. If he becomes bossy or demanding, Mindy will call him out on it. I've even seen him laugh it off and apologise – and get on with playing together.

Whatever she's got, I want to know the secret!

I said to Mindy's mum, "You know, I can't remember Precious ever having a really hard time around Mindy. I can't say he's ever had a full-blown meltdown with her around. Can you?" We've been friends since we were in high school, and our babies have grown up together – so we could put it down to that familiarity. But we couldn't think of a time when Precious had a sensory overload in Mindy's presence since they were toddlers.

Then I said to my friend "Oh, it's because Mindy is his *anchor*".

Although my friend looked a bit puzzled momentarily, she knows the look I get when something I say hasn't come from me. (We've been friends for eighteen years, she's well aware of how this works!) Spirit began to tell me that Mindy's energy had a grounding impact on my Precious, and the little girl who I've always said is an elemental, a little pixie – is surely an Earthly, **Anchoring** Soul. Her presence naturally calms, balances and stabilises the high frequency.

I discussed it with my friend and we shared a sentimental moment over the special bond between our children. As we watched them playing and laughing, each of them ignoring their respective siblings - it seemed so obvious! It was like they were speaking the same language and no one else in the room understood what the hell they were on about. It was gorgeous!

Over the next few weeks, during my interactions with people in general, Spirit would whisper randomly "Anchor. He's an anchor. She's an anchor". I started to get an idea of the types of souls who Spirit wanted to draw my attention to, people who appeared to be here (in a sense) to anchor the energy and to hold the light for other Souls. Some are children, and some are adults.

If I could sum up the similarities between them, I would describe 'Anchor' Souls as:

- Very down to earth – or Earthly Souls.
- Fairly even tempered, relaxed and not easily swayed.
- Can be slightly flamboyant or dramatic when in their most comfortable and natural state.
- They have a wisdom that exceeds 'book-smarts'.
- They have a natural ability for compassionate listening.
- They have a quirky and cheeky side, with a contagious sense of humour.
- Can be hot-tempered and broody when offended or hurt.

I realised that my few closest friends fit this description, and when I think of how I feel when they are around me or giving me counsel – I recognise that they are *my* Anchors. They help me to stay grounded, to level out and allow me to be myself – which is validating. It's a relief. It's homely – and it's something we all need. **There is an anchor for everyone, maybe more than one.** Someone that simply by being near – can pull your high flying, out of control and out of sorts energy – back to zero point. To balance the imbalance. There's little or no effort involved on their part, because it's not a conscious thing – it's energetic. It's magnetic. It's consciousness recognising consciousness, with unconditional love and acceptance.

Have a think about the people closest to you, in your own life. Who seems to make you feel more level headed once you've been near them? Who seems to just understand you, make you feel better without ever really *saying* anything at all? Who seems to just calm you down or put a stop to the nonsensical verbal vomit when you're having a self-pity-party? Let's consider your beautiful Precious, that amazing, high-vibrational, magical Soul. Who can you recognise as being *their* Anchor? Do they have one, or more? Are *you* their Anchor? More than likely, having been chosen by your Precious – you are their Anchor.

If you are not – you still can be an anchor for their energy.

Refer back to the previous chapter about Grounding. If you have done this, then you will naturally feel solid and become a beacon for them – they will seek you out because of how you *feel* to them. If you are solid and balanced, you are like a rock for them, a safe place that invites freedom and soothing relief. They may come to you, just to let it all out, because they know you can take it. They know you are unmovable and your love for them is unconditional. That's why you're The Chosen One.

If you are grounded in your own life, you are then able to come from a place of calm and solidarity, rather than one of matching anxiety and imbalance. (We all know how that ends, and it happens way more often than we'd care to admit.) With your grounded energy, your intuitive connection and your compassionate empathy for this Precious – you are now armed with a chance at being able to at least steady their energy with either a gentle touch, an embrace, or a listening ear.

Here's the thing about being an anchor – you don't need to fix anything. You don't need to have the magic words or the genius solution to be able to make an incredible difference in bringing some balance and calm into this child's energy. If you've done the hard work – you've recognised:

- *You* are A SOUL, *they* are a Soul, and you see their Divine Spark Within...
- They see the world very differently, and that is beautiful.
- They do not need to see things our way, we need to try to see things from their perspective.
- You know that *you* are The Chosen One, The Superhero's Superhero.
- You are also the Superhero of *your own* story...
- You have successfully grounded yourself in a way that is meaningful and powerful to you.

- That is enough. You are enough.

In case you skipped over that part or wanted to avoid it because you don't believe it, I'll repeat it again. **You are enough.** If you do nothing else in a day but *be there* after this work you have done – you have done your part.

*

We compare and judge ourselves. We pressure ourselves to do more FOR them. We look outside of ourselves for others to HELP them, to SAVE them.
We constantly struggle in silence and cry in exhaustion because we think that we are failing, like we are not GIVING enough.

Honey, all your Precious needs, is for you to take care of you first. Can't you see that?

I'm not saying ditch your family and run away to Thailand for six months to find yourself (although wouldn't that be nice?) I'm saying that instead of running yourself into the ground every day and giving every last inch of your sanity and energy to your kids – save some of that for *you*. You're no good to anyone if you're falling apart. You can't pour from an empty cup.

All of the answers you could ever need, are within you right now. You don't need to go anywhere or to buy anything to obtain or acquire it – it's all within that spectacular soul of yours. Self-healing is within your own capable hands. You just need to know how to call it out, you just need a catalyst for change – but you are the change you need.

Acceptance, release, surrender. If you need assistance to trigger that inner knowing, the innate ability to heal and know your Divinity and your purpose – put it out there to the Universe that you want the keys your freedom… and your path will marry up with that which you seek. It is already in front of you and it always has been, you just need to walk up and meet it. If you won't do the work for yourself, do it for your Precious – because he/she needs you to be you – the *real* you.

Affirmation

With my presence I am an anchor for love and light.

My love is a shield and I am firmly connected to all that is.

I stand strong for my Precious to use me as an anchor.

I am enough. I am enough. I am enough.

I am grateful for this wonderful, touching experience.

Chapter Sixteen

Siblings are Superheroes too

I often wonder what goes through the minds and hearts of the siblings of a soul who is on The Spectrum. This chapter is dedicated just to them, (more specifically my Little Precious) the subtle behind-the-scenes, integral piece of the puzzle. The warriors, the cheerleaders, the anchors. Those beautiful, wonderful souls who may feel invisible at times. I see you. We see you. We love you so much. You go with the flow, you are used to fitting in around the needs and schedule of your sibling – and I hope you know how incredible you are. How important you are. Your acceptance, patience and unconditional love of your sibling is awe-inspiring.

*

When My Precious was a toddler and had been diagnosed as being on The Autism Spectrum, I wondered whether I would ever have more children. I always imagined having a big family – especially being the third of four children in my own family, most of the women in my intermediate family had at least three to even seven or eight children. The diagnosis at first had me feeling as though I wouldn't be able to give My Precious the attention and care he needed if I had any more children, or that they would somehow miss out on the best part of me because I would always be 'distracted'. In my heart of hearts, I always wanted more than one child, not just because I'm naturally a maternal, nurturing person – but because I didn't want my child to be lonely or frankly… I didn't want him to be too spoiled!

I attended a workshop once where another parent said, "If I had my Autistic child first, I would never have had any more". I was surprisingly emotional about what was said, to the extent that I cried on the way home from the workshop. Although I understood what was meant by the comment, and that person had every right to say it – it upset me to think that I was so naïve to think that having another child was a good idea. It was upsetting that something as simple as 'having heaps of kids' in my family, may be that much more complicated for me… and that the decision may be unfair on My Precious, and any children to follow. It basically shot down my hopes and gave me a harsh reality check that shit might just be too damn hard.

So, I put it on the backburner. Whilst I was always very hands on with the Early Intervention therapies – I had an extra gusto, to put in the hard yards at the get-go to minimise Precious' struggles for the future. A future where if he could handle the world with more ease, it may allow us to have the energy, time and capacity to accommodate and broaden our lives for a sibling. As Precious grew, the world he lived in became more and more static and troublesome for him – and I began to think a second child would never be a viable option for us.

As I watched My Precious transcend through what I called the 'terrible threes' into a sweet and loving almost-four-year-old, it became obvious how lonely he was. He loved going to day-care, and it was always a treat to socialise with family and friends and other children – yet he would be truly sad when everyone had to leave. At that time, his dad and I decided we were all in a good place – and we felt ready to try to give him a little brother or sister. Although we were naturally concerned how he would cope with such a huge, life-altering transition, we understood his needs and were equipped to make the changes easier on him, to prepare him for what was to come.

Throughout the pregnancy – My Precious was educated on what was going on with mummy and why she was so sick all the time, and he was surprisingly more than understanding and empathetic. I found an app on my phone that had 3D simulation videos of what the baby would be doing at each weekly gestation, and this helped him to bond with the baby in utero… who he named 'Baby Jake' (a children's TV show about a young boy and his baby brother). We used Social Stories, a baby doll to pretend with, and encouraged him to feel the baby's movements and talk to him. He would hug my belly and tell the baby he loved him (even though we hadn't told him it was a boy, of course he already knew!)

As soon as My Little Precious was born and he met his new baby brother – it was love at first sight! Just when I thought my heart couldn't possibly cope with any more, it expanded with an explosion of unconditional love, and tears were shed the moment I saw My Precious' excitement and joy as he held his new brother. He loved baby so much, that at times he didn't know how to channel that overwhelming emotion. There were quite a few close calls – he didn't quite know how to be gentle, nor did he have much of a concept of personal space generally anyway – so during Little Precious' first year it was fairly stressful. Caution was needed at all times.

We enlisted the help of some emotional coaching story books to help with issues of jealousy and sharing mummy's attention and I made a giant photo book with a tailored story just for him – encouraging quiet voice, gentle touch, and accentuating the love and bond between them. This book helped shift his struggles like nothing else – using visuals of both personal photographs and iconic images and written instructions that rhymed, the book also showcased how special he was to his little brother, and vice-versa, as a beautiful keep-sake photo album.

Now, at ages almost seven and two and a half – these two are thick as thieves. My Little Precious is resilient – the bravest, most self-aware and thoughtful toddler I know. He is thrown around like a rag doll by his big brother and gets up shrieking for more like an excited little ninja on acid. Together they scale the furniture and torpedo onto the Kloudsac (therapeutic bean bag, a sensory item in our house) and roll all over each other on the floor cackling and laughing. They have their own language – like the call of the wild, My Precious shouts out "Ayaaa-ayaaa-ayaaaa" and Little Precious comes running (meanwhile I have been calling him by name for half an hour).

When one cries, so does the other. (I mean, not just crying - wailing like I just beat them over the head with a stick – all because the other one cried when I didn't let them eat a permanent marker.) My Little Precious has a tough time when My Big Precious has a sensory overload or an emotional meltdown, because they can be explosive, violent and very loud. They can be scary even for me, and I'm an adult. Poor Little Precious, trembling bottom lip and all, moseys on over to his big brother, arms outstretched and tries to give him a cuddle. "You otaay? What's da matter?" Sometimes – honestly – it's not safe. I have to remove him and focus on calming him down to tell him everything's alright. In those moments, he wraps his arms around my neck and hugs me so tight

– with tears coming down as he is both scared and compassionate for his brother. These moments tear at my heart. But – sometimes, probably more often than not – his hug and empathy alone, his bravery and resilience of getting right into the thick of it with arms outstretched – is enough to bring My Big Precious back down from his heightened state. It's enough to have us all hugging each other and giving each other tearful, sloppy kisses and apologies. He's just a dude. An absolute legend.

Most recently the mornings are the best. Both of the boys are still in their heavenly sleepy state, cute as a button and all gooey and lovely. I pop the kettle on to make my morning cuppa and warm milk for Little Precious and I hear teeny little conversation sneaking out of the room…

LP: "Good morning! Hab a gud sweep? You okay?"

MBP: "Good morning. I had a good sleep; did you have a good sleep?"

LP: "Ya. More Bottle?"

MBP: "Mum… wants his bottle. (Don't worry baby brudder, mum's coming.)"

LP: "Ya, Oooooh taaay. Tank yew."

MBP: "You're most welcome, you little cute baby. (Muuuuum...he's such a cute baby! How come he's so cute?")

LP: "Aw, you so tute!"

My Little Precious misses his big brother like crazy during school hours, and as soon as he sees him in the afternoon it's as though all of his Christmases have come at once! He follows him around like a shadow, and echoes everything he says (even the undesirables of course). The school hours give us a chance to have our own time though, and that is hugely important to us. Although I don't have nearly as much time doing activities and taking him on little adventures like I did when his brother was a little one, I have finally allowed myself to have a little cuddle and a nap on the couch with him every day. I look at my growing baby as he sleeps so angelically, and I just melt into gratitude. Thank you. Thank you for coming to us and blessing us with your shimmering light. Your smile melts my heart and we are so lucky to have you, to make our family complete.

For the last two nights when I am putting my Little Precious into bed for the night, my Big Precious has followed me so he can say goodnight properly too (which is a new thing, by the way). As he stands there looking into the cot, he has a sad smile on his face, and refuses to leave immediately. When we leave the room, he says to me, "I don't want to leave him, Mum.

Seeing him in his bed by himself makes me crying. Happy crying, I think – but I feel like I need to crying".

With my heart in my throat I put my arm around him and ask why he thinks he feels like crying. "Because I just love him so very much. I just love him. That's why." And with tears in his eyes and an uncomfortable smile, My Precious proves to me why I am so grateful I didn't give up on having another child. I am so grateful that Little Precious chose us, and he came here to anchor our energies and bring in such powerful loving and compassionate energy.

For the Big Precious – he has a best friend for life, a companion who loves him no matter what, and someone else to love no matter what. It's the most beautiful bond I have ever seen. I know that I personally wouldn't be myself without my siblings, and now that I watch my two ninjas zip around like two Tassie Devils destroying everything in the house, I am so content and proud knowing that they have each other.

This is my version of why my little one is a Sibling Superhero. If you have more than one child, whether they came before or after your child on The Spectrum or whether they are also on the Spectrum, you will have your own stories. Tell them, please. Every day. Tell them just how important and amazing they are – that they are special too. Thank them for choosing you and choosing to come here to be an anchor for their sibling.

Thank you, Sibling Superheroes. The Divine shower you with gratitude and loving energy, and your Mission here is not unnoticed. Not all Superheroes have capes, some have wings.

Addendum

During chapter fifteen, I delved into some challenging behaviour that My Precious was experiencing at the time of writing (which was about three months ago as I write this addendum). I felt it integral to add this part of the story here as it will show you the scope of the battle – ('try and try again' simply doesn't define what we go through to help our Superheroes overcome their challenges). It is also one of those lessons from Spirit that allows me to verify the process, to allow, receive and then put what I have received into practice and turn it into an experience. This is to be able to draw from these experiences to further explain the channelled messages herein and give you a tangible example. (As Maui from Moana would say, "You're Welcome!")

Now I'll be as delicate as I can with this, because in future I'm sure My Precious will read these words – and in no way is there any blame, anger, resentment or hard feelings towards him for what I'm about to explain. (I only have love in my heart – and gratitude for his tenacity and strength in overcoming such hurdles. There's also some Mummy Guilt but that doesn't serve any purpose, so we won't dwell on that!)

Without wanting to embarrass, shame or objectify him; it is necessary for you the reader (and for him, the reader in future) to know just how sensitive and vulnerable his energy is, how all Our Superheroes can be. It's a lesson to pay attention to the smaller things, and to advocate for what you think is best for your child as well. Although this is brutal honesty and I'm letting you in to some extremely private and personal stuff here, it is necessary for me to use our lives as examples to 'prove' if you will, that the messages about The View (p. 183) channelled from Spirit (for this book) are in fact extremely accurate. I *wrote* the shit and believe me I didn't fully comprehend what I was receiving until this happened. (Again, touché' Spirit – The Universe and the Almighty have really wowed me on this one, and that's not an easy feat!) Therein lies the point, I guess - so here goes.

*

My Precious was no longer himself... My sweet, sensitive, angelic and loving Superhero had become a ticking timebomb of violent outbursts and aggressive and emotional eruptions. He was increasingly irrational, irritated, miserable and fucking scary to be around, I'll admit. There were days where he would try to stab me (literally) with whatever he could get his hands on - from a drum stick, a ruler, an actual knife, broom handles, pens, wooden spoons or blunt elongated toys. There were days where he would punch and kick me in the stomach numerous times and come charging towards me with his hands out to claw at me – body slamming me to the ground (and by now he's over 40kg).

One day I even had to remove Little Precious from playing with him on the trampoline and lock the back door, watching him scream and pace around the back-yard throwing things at the doors and windows. All I could do was talk him down behind the safety of the glass until he calmed himself, but I didn't leave his sight. Why would I lock him out? Because he was wildly throwing his little brother around like a rag doll and when I tried to intervene, he grabbed his brother in a headlock and refused to let go. He needed to know that was *not* okay. I don't have to tell you, dear Soul, that I don't care what anyone thinks – I did what was best at the time and I know that you do what you must as well. (But hey, that's not grey in my hair – they're white-blonde highlights!)

This is *not* My Precious. Something was happening to him and I was at my wits end trying to figure it out. I'd tried EVERYTHING. Some things were working, some seemed to escalate things. No one particular 'treatment' solved the entire problem. Here's an overview of what I *did* try over the space of a couple of months.

- **Psychology**: Hysterical 'meltdowns' and violent outbursts in the therapy room, ending in using my own body as a therapeutic tool to stretch, lift and provide deep pressure for him. (Yeowie, he's bloody strong and heavy!)

- **A new bed**: Yep, assuming he was experiencing growing pains I purchased him a bed that is the same size as mine – a queen sized bed with Astrological themed bedding.

- **Energy reading/connecting with his Spark**: Refusal to connect with me resulting in aggression and emotional distress for getting too close (even from afar, my energy was felt and not appreciated.) His energy was so wired and open, absorbing everything and totally unbalanced.

- **Talking to him calmly or not at all** – Eventually raised voices seemed to be the best and most direct way of communicating (I know, right – yelling… well done super-mum. But if he can't hear amid the chaos in his mind and it snaps him out of it, you do what you have to).

- **Energy Healing**: He preferred physical touch rather than energy only, where I discovered the Unicorn and Dragon energy coming through instantly as I intuitively tapped in to what was needed. He enjoyed the deep pressure on his legs and lower body but nowhere else. This provided some relief, but only for a few days. He desperately needed grounding.

- **Dietary changes:** Disallowing sweet biscuits and desserts and replacing his choices with dry crackers and sweet fruit or frozen yoghurt. Education on good choices and healthy food options as well as a taste for fruit and the ability to try new things is on the up and up! One for the win!

- **GP:** Review for medical issues or physical ailments, revisiting Asthma medication and continence products. Discussed potential pain he may be experiencing for 'growing pains' and so forth. GP gave him a stern and honest lecture about how it's 'not cool' to hurt your mum and gave him a new preventer puffer that he can control himself – and it looks like a spaceship so, winning. (This dissolved the routine morning and evening meltdown as he refused his preventer medication and gave him some control back.)

- **Chiropractic**: For *both* of us. Not surprising, but this generally has instant results. The day after a cranial adjustment he began telling me messages from my dad – Precious was realigned to be able to access the Divine Realms and continue his amazing mediumship ability. As far as behaviour: this was improved for a few days' – tops; but can be revisited when needed.

- **Emotional Coaching:** Daily encouragement for communication and the addition of a 'journal' that he could draw his feelings in. Communication somewhat improved, and I began to see the general expressions on his stick figures were angry and scary. The fact that he was willing and volunteering to journal most days was a very big step in the right direction and gave me an insight into what he was going through without him having to think too hard or 'talk' about his feelings.

- **Sensory Diet:** Adding jumping, crashing, crawling, stretching and oral input/output (use of bubbles and straws) had to be well-hidden because the slightest inkling that there was some 'work' involved resulted in a standoff. Heavy work was introduced using a novelty back pack filled with a rice bag once or twice, before he was too clever and saw through it!

- **Meditation:** I dug out the old meditation CDs from his earlier years and it was no surprise that the Songs of the Dolphins was his first and lasting choice, before choosing a guided meditation for children. He began to sleep better and woke feeling much more refreshed.

- **From 'limiting' screen time to a *complete* iPad/PlayStation ban:** This caused some major challenges – but things got worse before eventually getting better and achieving amazing results! This was probably the most important change of all, especially after an early diagnosis and the first thing the clinicians told us was to "buy him an iPad". That's a lifelong habit right there, but man have we learned some valuable lessons about screen time.

- **Planned Ignoring:** I realised that I needed to pick my battles wisely, not just for his sake – but for my own as well. Surprisingly this became my go-to because the lack of reaction caused him to self-analyse and eventually think about his behaviour before telling me he *wanted* to talk about it.

- **Worm treatment:** It was suggested to me through the Autism Superheroes support group I run, that worms can cause irritability and behavioural issues – so it was worth a shot! I can't say for certain whether it worked for Precious, but it did for Little Precious!

- **Good old-fashioned discipline:** An overhaul of his reward systems, with stricter consequences. Clear rules, warning, consequence and action. This most definitely involved removing the child into a safe space. As you can imagine trying to get a heavy, stubborn seven – year – old to his bedroom requires some heavy lifting and occasional dragging and heaving. (Thank God for my chiropractor!)

- **Streamlining school, two homes, and goals in multiple therapies: advocacy.**
    - I left notes in his diary, begging his teachers for some support or input, any inkling of what he was like at school – and by all reports it was just happening at home. They were happy to see me for a one on one to discuss and together we worked on a plan. This was imperative.
    - I cried to his father that we need to work together (despite our separation

and very different parenting styles). I insisted on the dire need for streamlined routine across the board and a united front on the rules and consequences. Communication between us needed to be clear and honest – no games, the greater good was the children's best interests. We are now working together, and things are running very smoothly.

- **Lack:** Limiting all forms of rewards including visitors, outings, park trips, movies, games, special dinners - I couldn't even throw him a birthday party, because any slight reward or treat allowed this behaviour to escalate. (Compared to my childhood – my kids are spoiled for no damn reason. This was probably long overdue!)

By the second month of this I was exhausted, devastated, and terrified. I could see that he was in pain, he was sorry, and he was stuck in another world that he just couldn't seem to escape from. It was painful for me too, that I couldn't seem to find anything that could relieve this for him, was so much worse than anything he'd done to physically or verbally hurt me.

At night I always try to sit with him a moment and let the woes of the day fall away and get all sweet and lovey-dovey, so we don't ever go to bed angry. Most of the time during those few months, I couldn't achieve that. Occasionally I couldn't even bring myself to say goodnight until he was asleep. Do you understand how heartbreaking that is? I was beginning to hate myself a little bit every day, because the constant struggle was driving me to parenting-breaking point where I was the 'psycho-bitch' that I used to see in my mum when I was a kid. (I'm sorry Mum, I think I get it now!)

One night I sat on his bed and cried, as he shouted at me and carried on for the thousandth time that day. I faced away from him as I cried, and suddenly My Precious stopped his incessant nagging and foul attitude rebuttals. He put his hands on my back and I flinched away, when he said "Mum... Mummy? Why are you crying? Do you want a hug, *or what*? Sometimes when 'Little Precious' cries, he hugs me, and it looks like it makes him better. So... you want a hug, *or what*?"

Despite the abruptness – I looked at him and said, "Yes. Yes please". He asked me what was wrong, and I explained that I didn't want to yell – I was sick of the yelling all the time, I didn't know what to do anymore and that I was just so sad that I was failing. He forced my head onto his little chest and said, "Mummy you just have to calm down, take a deep breath. Gotta get your energy back, okay? Just get your dragon to get your energy back".

Holy shit. Pepe. My dragon. Transmutation – THAT is what he was talking about.
(*There's* my sweet boy, he's still in there somewhere!)

Those moments where he could see my vulnerability, that his actions were affecting me - allowed him a space to feel empathy and to allow the voice of the divine to come through. (It is a common notion that people on The Spectrum lack empathy – but for My Precious I find that he is incredibly empathetic.) Seeing me like this touched him right in the feels and pushed through a lot of the other stuff he was feeling.

After that night, each time his behaviour or emotion escalated he began to apologise during those philosophical moments at bedtime – he'd enter a period of reflection and tell me that he didn't know *why* he was behaving this way, and that he can't help it. He began to get upset that he was a 'bad kid' or a 'horrible person' and these are never words that he hears from us at home. *Not ever.* Absolutely heartbreaking, that my little boy couldn't help his behaviour and was believing that he was a bad person.

Because it seemed like a relatively *gradual* downward spiral, it was as though the moment I completed this book, everything seemed to fall apart. It was as though I was being punished – my ego telling me I was too cocky, that I assumed to know more than I do – or that I am not able to go ahead with the publication of this book because I couldn't get a handle on my own kid. Who was I to preach to people about how to 'be' or give them any inch of sound advice when I was dealing with the extreme opposite of what I had been trying to achieve? I must be a fraud! I must be full of shit and no one likes me, everybody hates me, I think I'll go and eat some worms... (I can be a drama-llama sometimes, but I'm real – remember?)

I didn't stay in that state of mind very long though, because, well – ain't nobody got time for dat. I pulled my head out of my ass and started to pay close attention to his triggers – and more so to the ranting and raving, the topics that he seemed to obsess over which in turn caused some type of 'freak out' soon after. I made time to research some stuff that he would talk about, and was absolutely mortified to realise that these games, apps, YouTube videos and walkthroughs were not age appropriate **at all.**

When I saw a videogame called 'Granny' that depicted an old woman in a nightgown covered in blood and wielding a knife – I almost burst into tears. There were what I had thought were music videos that I caught glimpses of him watching over time that when watched completely were actually brutal and violent themed animations with some cool music in the background (Bendy and the Ink Machine, Five Nights of Freddie, and other horror-bul stuff that made my jaw drop). He had gone from watching rich kids open fucking Kinder Surprise Eggs and toys to watching nightmare inducing shit that makes MY skin crawl!

EPIC PARENTING FAIL. I tried everything but one thing. Paying fucking attention.

As sobering and shameful as this realisation was at the time, at least it gave me a Segway into a discussion about cyber safety and what the rules are for what is appropriate viewing (all of which I know we've discussed many times, but this was cause for more attention). He hadn't had access to the iPad or gaming consoles of any kind for at least two weeks when I noticed a slight change in his behaviour over the weekends, which was a major breakthrough! By Monday after school it would escalate again, and the pattern began to rinse and repeat. After some detective work and some reverse psychology, it was apparent that although he wasn't accessing this material at home anymore – he still had access to it at school, on the bus and any time we'd visit friend's houses on their devices.

I tried to empower him to make good choices, to stick to our family rules even if other children don't have the same rules in their house, and basically allowed him to take responsibility for his own choices and actions. I explained to him that the horror and scary images and videos he was exposing himself to were attaching lower energy (or bad energy) to him, and because he is so beautiful and sensitive that he needed to protect his energy from that stuff. I told him he is like his mum, and that we must be careful what we let ourselves get into because we can be magnets for stuff that's not of love, and that makes us feel yucky and angry.

Wouldn't you know it, the boy began to understand me. (He doesn't understand emotion so much, but you talk to him about energy and he completely comprehends.) My poor boy was living in a video game, in a context he couldn't separate from reality – and between peer pressure and his intent focus on what he likes, he was absolutely lost between realities. As I began to get a little closer to finding the problems – I could finally begin to work on some solutions.

It wasn't until I sat at my kitchen table during a one on one consultation with My Precious' Occupational Therapist that I began to rattle off some of the techniques and things that I had tried that seemed to be helping to improve things, yet there was no <u>one</u> thing that seemed to be a silver bullet. I explained that I felt like he needed to try less mainstream things such as sound healing and perhaps get him into a robotics class - and that I had purchased him a free-standing hammock for his birthday. As I explained the reason for my purchase – I said that I felt he would like to be suspended when he was having a hard time, and then it hit me…

Like a crazy person, I flew away from the kitchen table (the therapist probably thinking I was a whack job) and grabbed a copy of this very book that I had printed and bound after sending my first draft off to the editor. I flicked through to The View, where I specifically remembered writing something about being 'suspended'. (See, although I wrote that section and I understood what I was writing, I hadn't yet put it into perspective with practice.) In front of the therapist I re-read *my own book* and almost fell off my chair as I read out the paragraph.

"Innate knowledge of concepts far beyond typical Earthly perceptions and ideas... Intense mood swings and episodes of unexplained sadness, apathy and depression following a cosmic or global event (even if they are consciously unaware.)"

Interestingly – I understood at the time we were experiencing a leap, a frequency upgrade in the consciousness of the planet – 'The Collective'. I had been going through the motions as an Intuitive and an Empath, so it's not at all surprising that I found the helpful information under the title of **Layer #5. Cosmic/Collective Consciousness.** It was here that I read on aloud and was blown away with how intense and accurate the information previously channelled was in real time - to us in the NOW.

I began laughing and smiling, as though a light bulb had just turned on and I had in my hand the answers to all the questions I had been asking myself. So – I will explain it like this: I looked at the chapter labelled: 'The View - Part Two' and assessed what My Precious scored in each Energy Layer and Energy Hub. Using a basic score system, I was able to determine that My Precious scored 5/6 with imbalances in **Layer #5. Cosmic/Collective Consciousness.** (Some of the Complimentary Energies were already in place and were working to benefit My Precious.)

To make things easier to evaluate – for you the reader, I decided to add each layer into an easily assessable format as follows, using my story as an example.

Symptoms of imbalance or heightened energy perception/regulation (May present as challenges)	Complimentary Energies
Special interest or fascination with space, planets, stars and solar system	Akashic Records and Past Life Readings (possibly regression rituals)
May present with the ability to use technology far beyond the typical capability of their age group	Healing with divine coding
May present with the ability to take complex electronics apart and put them back together	Sound Healing (Crystal/Tibetan Singing Bowls, Binaural/Isochronic Tones)
Special interests within the topics of science, physics, mathematics, computer coding and robotics	Numerology and Astrological studies
Innate knowledge of concepts far beyond typical Earthly perceptions and ideas	Limit exposure to technology and electromagnetic frequency (especially in sleep areas)
Intense mood swings and episodes of unexplained sadness, apathy and depression following a cosmic or global event (even if they are consciously unaware)	Regular physical exercise to burn off excess energy that stores after downloading constantly (may like balancing, suspending/hanging and being high off the ground)

Not surprisingly, he scored 6/6 within the **Energy Hub - The View.** Just by looking at these charts you can already see based on what I have explained – what worked and what didn't, that this information (whether I was consciously aware or not) was the answer to my woes at the time, and the explanation behind some of the unexplained behaviours and moods.

Symptoms of imbalance or heightened energy perception/regulation (*May present as challenges*)	Complimentary Energies
Frustration and anger outbursts	Sensory Regulation – tailored sensory diet
Confusion and lack of concentration	Energy balancing using Unicorn and Dragon energies (Feminine and Masculine – gentle energy for this particular healing)
Switching focus from one subject to another rapidly	Sound-boarding: being able to let the child have open conversations and share experiences that may be obscure or 'other-worldly' (venting/unburdening is important)
Emotional overwhelm or complete sensory shutdown	Creative outlet
Physical aches and pains with no medical explanation	Limited processed foods and refined sugar
The need to shut off from affection and interaction (when there may be a jamming of signals at the centre point and any further input is overwhelming)	Yoga, Meditation, Swimming, Tai Chi, Qigong

I was able to look up the Complimentary Energies – to find ideas that would benefits or help My Precious balance his energy and to understand what he was going through energetically *as well as* what was going on physically and emotionally.

I must have intuitively been tapping into the messages from Spirit that were written in this book, which in turn helped me to return to it as a guide to help me to help my son. Not only that, but I now had an example of how The View can be used for my readers – and to tell you that it works, and I have added a section at the back of the book that is set out for a quick guide to allow you to use The View this simple way. I trust that this is what Spirit meant the information to be used for, and I am grateful for the lesson (although, it was in no way a pleasant experience, I see now it was for the Greater Good).

After this realisation, I took my copy of this book to My Precious' school when I had a meeting with his teachers. They were beautifully open and accepting of my unorthodox views and allowed me to discuss my concerns and expectations regarding my child's cyber safety and exposure to inappropriate material. They too were mortified about the material that the children had been accessing and immediately acted to rectify the problem inhouse. (These children are so clever that they have been able to get around the parental controls and blocks both at home and school, so we all need to be vigilant in this regard.) I couldn't have been happier that I was validated, and together we came up with a set of personalised rules for My Precious to use at home – with a visual chart that needed to be ticked off and sent to the teacher daily. Failure to achieve the tasks meant his teachers would be notified and the consequences rolled out in school as well as at home.

With a combination of all these exploratory measures, some heart and soul searching and advocacy – achievement unlocked! We got there in the end! I could have saved myself a lot of time and heartache and physical injury (and energy for My Precious) if I had been able to utilise The View at the first sign of imbalance. But you see, there are many lessons here for us – and I am more than ecstatic to report that since using the combination, tailored, child-specific approach as well as my own connection with my child and intuition, I now have my sweet, sensitive, angelic and loving Superhero back... the wiser, more empowered and upgraded version.

I am so grateful for this experience, and the growth that has occurred.

May you learn from my example and be armed with some tools and guidance to approach future challenges with understanding, love, ease and grace.

A Parting Word from the Author

Dear, wonderful, powerful Soul.

Congratulations, you have made it to the end of this first instalment of Autism Superheroes: The Spark Within! Thank you for showing up, for yourself and for your Precious darlings. May you now be different, having experienced a meaningful shift in perspective since you have read these words. May the words have had a tremendous positive impact on your life. I see you in a high esteem in my mind and in my heart, I love you, and I believe in you. You have the power to move mountains and the impact you have on your children's lives is incredible. You are incredible. Don't ever forget it.

About this book

Spirit has guided me through the entire process of writing this book, and I want to accredit my 'Entourage' for the service I was able to provide with their loving Grace. I am merely a servant of the Light - without Source, I would not have the clarity or ability to achieve this Mission. Many blessings, love and gratitude to The One, for choosing me to be the messenger.

*

I was 'given' the title of each chapter to this book, before I had even started writing it. I was then (for the most part) left to my own devices to draw from my experience to fill them in as I wanted. At the beginning, it was only every so often that Spirit would lean in and drop in a few words and concepts – or give me a nudge. No one was more surprised than I, when my creative writing was intercepted by Spirit – and suddenly turned from anecdotal to completely intuitive channellings at times! I had no idea this was going to be so informative and ground breaking – and I am amazed and grateful for the experience and privilege to have been able to deliver this information for you (and to learn for myself for the first time too!)

It seems that the named chapters I was given at the beginning were a prelude, a Segway for me to be able to receive the messages from the Divine in this way. With the support of Spirit and my passion and enthusiasm for assisting those high frequency souls on the Autism Spectrum – it was with ease and grace I have enjoyed this journey.

During the last few chapters that were added spontaneously (as guided by Spirit) I felt the intensity of the energy (that even had me astonished and taken aback!) Spirit had begun to take over and I have merely been the vessel. My job was to put the information I was given down on paper, for you to see. I have stepped aside and allowed the energy to work through me. I gave what I got. It doesn't always make sense at first, but everything falls into alignment eventually.

With the power and detail that has been coming through, I know it is a lot to take in – and in the interest of avoiding overwhelming you with too much information too quickly – I will leave you with an open ending to this book. Spirit has advised that this is one of a three part series, that will correlate to the energy of the time frame it each is written in. In the next instalment I am being guided to delve deeper into the aspects of Energy Healing, as well as the intricate details of the spiritual gifts that one on the Autism Spectrum may possess. We will cover past lives and Akashic Records, psychic development and more. We will go on an in-depth journey into how to utilise your connection and the layered energy system (The View) to develop a balancing technique for your Precious and take a deeper look into the Divine Realms. (My favourite!)

Gratitude

Firstly, I want to recognise my two children, my Precious Ones – whom I absolutely adore and admire. My boys have given me the inspiration and drive to be the best version of me I can be; not just for them but for my own soul evolution. They amaze me every day, and no words can describe the love I have for these two miracles and blessings. My heart and Soul explode with oceans of love, and I cherish every moment – even when my patience is tested, they are my everything.

My Big Precious – Thank you for choosing me, and for blessing our lives every day. You are an inspirational, gifted spiritual being and thank you for allowing me to share your story to help other children and parents. Your courage and tenacity amaze me, and I love you to infinity and beyond. You have raised my consciousness – just by entering the world, and as it increases, my wish is to continue to grow and develop alongside you. I look forward to watching you continue to do so for the rest of the world.

My Little Precious – Thank you for choosing me and blessing our lives every day. You have come into this world as a warrior, an anchor for your brother and a beam of cheeky happiness that lights up a room. Your strength and patience are overwhelmingly beautiful, and your ability to just roll with the flow of our often chaotic and busy lives is simply amazing. I love you to infinity and beyond and thank you for choosing to be here for your big brother and the gorgeous bond that you share. Your joyful, playful energy reminds me to stop and smell the roses, to get in touch with my inner child – and that it's okay to play. (A gift in this hectic world!)

I have a long list of 'advisors'…

My big sister Bel - We have been through the trenches together, and you are one of the few closest to a mother figure to my boys, and to me sometimes. Thank you for filling the role of Big Sister, Parent and Grandparent (who still looks younger than her little sister mind you) and words can't express my gratitude for having you in my life. Love you, thank you Sistoir!

My Sisters from other-misters - Jess, Lisa & Crystal, and my Wench Craig: You each play a completely different role in my life – and yet I would not be me without each of you. From listening to me dribble, to sage advice, and sometimes a reality check – I appreciate your amazing energy and contribution not just to my life – but the lives of my boys. Soul family. Love you guys to bits!

Crodge, you know what you mean to me. Thank you for giving me the support and encouragement to keep going – even when I am a pain in the butt. Never have I known the love, empowerment and unwavering support than what you have shown me. You celebrate my quirkiness and encourage my uniqueness, allowing me to be my most authentic self. Fireworks and stuff.

You're my people. You have always supported me, and specifically in the last twelve months as I have transformed my life – you have been there through the toughest and best times. You've been my sounding board and cheered me on at the sidelines from the very beginning. You know me to be the eccentric and quirky one and have always celebrated me for it. Thanks for putting up with my verbal vomit and incessant ranting and long-winded stories! I cannot express the love and gratitude I have for all that you have done and continue to do for me and my babies, and I wouldn't be me without you.

Shane - Thank you for everything in the earlier years, that have helped shape who I have become. Thank you for everything as we co-parent our two beautiful boys. We have managed to create two wonderful human beings. No matter what, we did good.

To Mum - Thank you for seeing my spiritual potential as a child and reminding me often – even if it embarrassed me. Since your passing I was able to connect with my mediumship abilities, and you have shown me without a doubt that there is proof of life after death. Thanks for pestering me all the time!

To Dad - Thank you for encouraging and supporting me to be a fair and just parent – to discipline with love and balance. For your religious knowledge and your unwavering faith in God – my original Spiritual teacher. Most of all, for the amazing bond you shared with My

Precious. Thank you for showing him you're still around too.

To all of my other family who have and continue to help me to be the best parent and person I can be, who make up the community that love my children and celebrate their milestones and wins with me: Tim & Ash, Jeremy, Aunty Chel & Uncie Morgs (and co!) Nay-Nay and Zay-Zay! Lisa & Dave.

Professionals who helped us get to where we are today:

Becky N: The original OT who started it all (my favourite, we love you!)

Maddie P: The most energetic and personable young superstar OT

Mikayla M: Talented and 'real' Speechy and fellow Mumma Bear.

Sam & Tess: Teachers, mentors. You guys are so important to our Superheroes, and you're changing the future every day. What truly amazing humans you and your colleagues are. Thank you!

Special thanks to Michael Mackintosh and Arielle Hecht for your continuous love, support, guidance and mentorship at Awakened Academy

www.awakenedacademy.com

Resources

Resources

- **"3 Seconds to Being Your Higher Self"** (Book) By Arielle Hecht
- Reference to Sensory Processing Disorder: https://childdevelopment.com.au/areas-of-concern/diagnoses/sensory-processing-disorder-spd

Resources and Recommended Courses

- **"More Than Words" Hanen Program**
  http://www.hanen.org/Programs/For-Parents/More-Than-Words.aspx
- **"The Autism MOOC" (Massive Open Online Course) – Swinburne University**
  https://www.swinburne.edu.au/study/options/find/online/autism-mooc/
- **"Tuning Into Kids" Emotional Coaching** (Parenting class locally organised by a City Council)
- **"The Traffic Jam In My Brain"** (A Sensory Processing Approach to Challenges Associated with Autism, ADHD, Learning and Behavioural Disorders) – Genevieve

Jereb OT
https://shop.sensorytools.net/tjb/index.html
- **The Zones of Regulation** (Book)
  By Leah Kuypers

Images

- All images owned by the author
- 'The View' Graphics and Cover Design by Lisa Hein: Evolution Design Agency
  https://www.evolutiondesign.com.au/

The View

Quick Guide & Score Check

NOTE: 'The Complimentary Energies' sections are in no specific order or relationship to a specific 'Symptom of Imbalance' in the following tables. These suggestions are to be used as a guide only, and you are encouraged to use your own intuition towards ideas that are suitable for your child.

1. The Physical Realm

- ❖ This is the densest, harshest energy that The Soul experiences.
- ❖ This is what we can **see physically** around us – the third dimension.
- ❖ Perceived by the five senses: sound, smell, sight, taste, touch.
- ❖ This energy is rigid and often hard to endure for the high frequency soul.
- ❖ It is hard to endure because the low-density energy does not transmit well, it is hard to compute or translate into a high enough vibration and becomes *distorted* input to the Soul.
- ❖ It is as if the signal is being sent from old technology into new technology.

Symptoms of imbalance or heightened energy perception/regulation *(May present as challenges)*	Complimentary Energies:
Over sensitivity to sound	Gentle energy healing modalities that *do not* require physical touch
Over sensitivity to touch	Meditation and chakra balancing
Over sensitivity to visual stimulation	Earthly grounding rituals (physical grounding techniques)
Over sensitivity to over-population or crowded spaces	Working with, healing or exposure to the Fae, (Fairies) Mermaid and Dolphin Realms.
Preferring to play or be alone	Desensitisation/sensory regulation (with guidance from a trained professional)
Over sensitivity to temperature	Eating wide variety of grounding foods (e.g. root vegetables)
Seeks out extremes with diet (bland, crunchy, or salty and sweet.)	Sound healing
Oral fixations or phobias (particularly with teeth brushing and food textures/temperatures)	

SCORE_____ / 8

1. Energy within the Physical Realm

- This may be perceived as a sixth or Psychic Sense.
- A heightened sense of FEELING is perceived in this energy field.
- Relates to the field of energy frequency emitted by *what is within* the physical (energy from people, animals, earth, inanimate objects. The elements – Earth, air, fire, water.)
- This energy is higher frequency than the third dimension (physical) and is easier to understand and perceive for the sensitive soul.
- It gives clearer input and direct explanation to The Soul's innate perceptions. (It speaks in a language the Soul can interpret naturally, it's turned up a notch on the dial of high energy so to speak.)

Symptoms of imbalance or heightened energy perception/regulation *(May present as challenges)*	Complimentary Energies:
Under-sensitivity to sound	Energy healing using gentle, subtle energies with or without the use of touch sensation
Under-sensitivity to touch	Deep pressure on the imbalanced areas of the body
Under-sensitivity to visual stimulation	Working with, healing or exposure to Unicorn and Angelic Realms
Picking up on other people's feelings and moods	Meditation
Awareness of future events before they happen (premonitions and psychic ability)	Sound healing/therapy: High frequency sounds (such as dolphins, binaural beats)
Empathy – feeling other people's feelings and displaying the emotions of others	Music and movement
Lack of spatial awareness, or 'feeling the edges in space' (Because they are so in touch with energy it is often the case that they are clumsy or find the human body difficult to get used to)	May benefit from regular, light meals – fresh fruit and salad vegetables

SCORE_____ / 7

2. Time

- This is a non-linear perspective of time.
- Time is seen as an infinity symbol rather than a straight line.
- This perception gives the ability to see different time lines at once.
- To alter the timeline in the now, ripples change throughout the entire view of time – and so there can be difficulty in 'resetting' the paradigm after an unprecedented change has occurred.
- A bird's eye view or 'eagle eye'.

Symptoms of imbalance or heightened energy perception/regulation *(May present as challenges)*	Complimentary Energies:
Struggle to comprehend 'time' in a 3D/linear way	Working with, healing or exposure to the Dragon Realms and Ascended Masters (St. Germaine, Melchizedek)
Distress, anxiety and overwhelm when timelines and plans are disrupted	Mindfulness meditation
The need for a detailed plan with specific detail	Yoga
Extremely accurate memory	Use of 'timer' and daily schedule, visual aids and Social Stories
Photographic and visual memory and the need for visuals to plan for future events	

SCORE_____ / 5

3. Divine Realms

- ❖ Another non-linear perspective.
- ❖ A 'bubble-like' dimension or layer of energy.
- ❖ Infinity symbol rather than a flat dimension or world.
- ❖ This realm spins parallel to the 'Time' energy, as if two perfectly balanced infinity symbols are consistently spinning evenly.
- ❖ When in balance and unison: they spin together at one central point.
- ❖ This is the realm of Divine interdimensional energies such as Angels, Unicorns, Dragons, Fairies/elementals, Spirit guides, Extra-terrestrials, Lost Souls and Departed Souls.
- ❖ This is an extremely high frequency energy, made up of codes that the Soul naturally understands and deciphers. (Like a native language)
- ❖ The Soul is constantly 'tapped into' or 'hooked up' to this realm and can communicate energetically, telepathically and send and receive messages and healing with ease.
- ❖ This is potentially the most comfortable of the energies for this Soul, as he/she remembers what it was like to reside there without physical form.

Symptoms of imbalance or heightened energy perception/regulation *(May present as challenges)*	Complimentary Energies:
May stare off in 'trance' like state for long periods	Regular energetic clearing and balancing techniques and rituals
Ability to sense the Spirit world (see, hear, feel high frequencies)	Shielding and connection with Angels and personal Spirit/Animal Guides
Talks to or plays with 'imaginary' friends	Yoga and Meditation – this soul is most likely a Yogi and may experience profound visions during dreams and meditations – take note!
Fascination or special interest with mystical creatures (fairies, dragons, unicorns etc)	Daily mantras and positive affirmations
Communicates with loved ones in the Spirit World (talks as though someone in Spirit is joining the conversation)	Spiritual guidance, counselling or coaching: lots of support
Sees orbs or 'bubbles' of energy	Journaling
May present with phobias or fears of 'monsters' or speak about mythical creatures as if they are tangible 'real' beings	Chakra balancing and aura clearing

SCORE_____ / 7

5. Cosmic / Collective Consciousness

- ❖ This relates to the Cosmos, the Universe, the consciousness of all that is.
- ❖ This is a collective energy that is an integration of all living beings – the overall 'oneness' of all.
- ❖ The Soul can feel, see and download the collective consciousness information and data – as well as to balance, contribute, transmute and send healing to this life force energy.

Symptoms of imbalance or heightened energy perception/regulation *(May present as challenges)*	Complimentary Energies:
Special interest or fascination with space, planets, stars and solar system	Akashic Records and Past Life Readings (possibly regression rituals)
May present with the ability to use technology far beyond the typical capability of their age group	Healing with divine coding
May present with the ability to take complex electronics apart and put them back together	Sound Healing (Crystal/Tibetan Singing Bowls, Binaural/Isochronic Tones)
Special interests within the topics of science, physics, mathematics, computer coding and robotics	Numerology and Astrological studies
Innate knowledge of concepts far beyond typical Earthly perceptions and ideas	Limit exposure to technology and electromagnetic frequency (especially in sleep areas)
Intense mood swings and episodes of unexplained sadness, apathy and depression following a cosmic or global event (even if they are consciously unaware)	Regular physical exercise to burn off excess energy that stores after downloading constantly (may like balancing, suspending/hanging and being high off the ground)

SCORE_____ / 6

The View: The Central Point

- ❖ This is the central point, the crux of everything.
- ❖ This is the control centre for interpreting the energies in their inner and outer world.
- ❖ The knowing point – where everything makes sense on a soul level.
- ❖ Where everything energetic enters and can be interpreted, sorted out and filtered.
- ❖ The central point where everything meets: a 'traffic' hub where everything connects and filters traffic in and out.
- ❖ Perception, understanding and healing through their heart space.
- ❖ Integrity is felt through this energy centre.

Symptoms of imbalance or heightened energy perception/regulation (May present as challenges)	Complimentary Energies:
Frustration and anger outbursts	Sensory Regulation – tailored sensory diet
Confusion and lack of concentration	Energy balancing using Unicorn and Dragon energies (Feminine and Masculine – gentle energy for this particular healing)
Switching focus from one subject to another rapidly	Sound-boarding: being able to let the child have open conversations and share experiences that may be obscure or 'other-worldly' (venting/unburdening is important)
Emotional overwhelm or complete sensory shutdown	Creative outlet
Physical aches and pains with no medical explanation	Limited processed foods and refined sugar
The need to shut off from affection and interaction (when there may be a jamming of signals at the centre point and any further input is overwhelming)	Yoga, Meditation, Swimming, Tai Chi, Qigong

SCORE_____ / 6

The Spark

- Where the soul resides within the physical body.
- (This spark is inside all living beings.) Zero Point.
- The soul is driving the vessel, it is pure love, joy, bliss and creation.
- All lifetimes and lessons, karmic records and knowledge is stored here.
- If all energies are in alignment the Spark has a communication with the View. (There exists an energetic life force between them to transmit and decode all input so as the 'world' makes sense.)
- If there is no connection or a skewed connection, Time and Divinity are off balance which stagnates and causes static and poor flow within The View.

Symptoms of imbalance or heightened energy perception/regulation *(May present as challenges)*	Complimentary Energies:
May display severe challenges and delays with speech and comprehension of instructions if the Spark is disconnected from the View	Meditation and mindfulness practice
The ability to 'zone out' into a peaceful state with little effort (if all is in alignment)	Bathing in gentle sunlight and swimming in natural water
Intense connection to other high frequency souls with little or no communication	Karmic balancing and healing
Places the forehead against things, people or animals that they like	Unburdening, venting, creative expression
May display tendencies to hit their forehead or head-bang to relieve numbness, aching or disconnection	Swimming, martial arts, barefoot walking (grounding)
	Puzzles and mathematics
	Systems and computer coding

SCORE _____ / 5

Physical Feeling & Healing

- ❖ The sensation of touch is heightened, or under sensitive.
- ❖ A soul may feel the energy of all the combining fields with the use of their hands and fingers.
- ❖ Through the hands and fingers there are receptors to decode and transfer solid/dense (3D) information into higher frequency that can be absorbed, comprehended and expressed, acting as a filtration system.
- ❖ The expression of emotion flows through the hands and can often result in mannerisms that need constant input or pressure to be expressed or relieved.
- ❖ The intense energy of this soul of a healing nature can have profound calming and healing properties when used for this intention.

Symptoms of imbalance or heightened energy perception/regulation *(May present as challenges)*	Complimentary Energies:
'Flapping' and irregular finger flicking or tapping movements and mannerisms	Sensory Diet and integration/regulation
Other self-stimulating using the hands and fingers	Working with and healing from the Archangels (Archangel Raphael, Archangel Michael and Archangel Christiel) and Fairies
The need to touch and feel things in order to understand or learn	Yoga, Meditation, Swimming, Tai Chi, Qigong
The tendency to squeeze things that they like or dislike, as a way to interpret these feelings	Earthly sensory activities (gardening, playing outside)
Having a calming or soothing effect on someone with their touch	Sound healing and balancing
Difficulty refining fine motor skills such as handwriting and using control over their fingers to complete small tasks	Companions such as household pets
Oversensitive or under sensitive to hands being wet, dirty, sticky, dry etc	

SCORE_____ **/ 7**

White Light
PUBLISHING

www.ingramcontent.com/pod-product-compliance
Lightning Source LLC
Chambersburg PA
CBHW071859290426
44110CB00013B/1208